FOR ORGANS, PIANOS & ELECTRONIC KEYBOARDS

E-Z PLAY TODAY

234

2nd EDITION

Disney

LOVE SONGS

ISBN 978-1-5400-3530-1

E-Z Play ® TODAY Music Notation © 1975 HAL LEONARD LLC
E-Z PLAY and EASY ELECTRONIC KEYBOARD MUSIC are registered trademarks of HAL LEONARD LLC.

Visit Hal Leonard Online at
www.halleonard.com

Contact Us:
Hal Leonard
7777 West Bluemound Road
Milwaukee, WI 53213
Email: info@halleonard.com

In Europe contact:
Hal Leonard Europe Limited
Distribution Centre, Newmarket Road
Bury St Edmunds, Suffolk, IP33 3YB
Email: info@halleonardeurope.com

In Australia contact:
Hal Leonard Australia Pty. Ltd.
4 Lentara Court
Cheltenham, Victoria, 3192 Australia
Email info@halleonard.com.au

Beauty and the Beast
from BEAUTY AND THE BEAST

Registration 1
Rhythm: Ballad

Music by Alan Menken
Lyrics by Howard Ashman

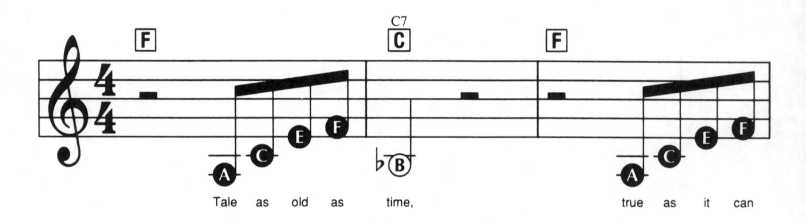

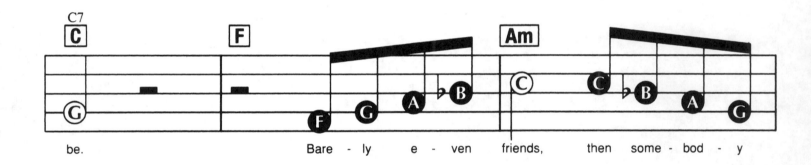

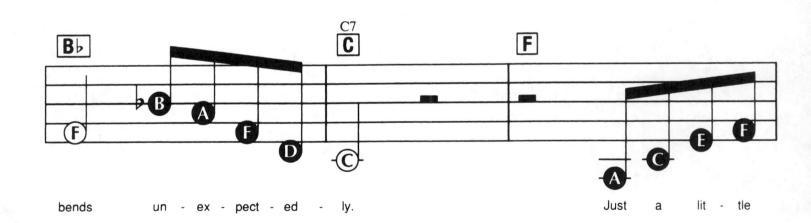

3

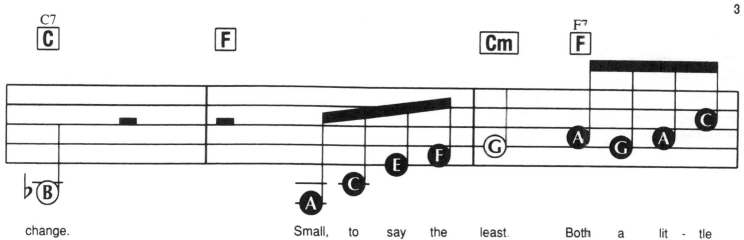

change.   Small, to say the least. Both a lit - tle

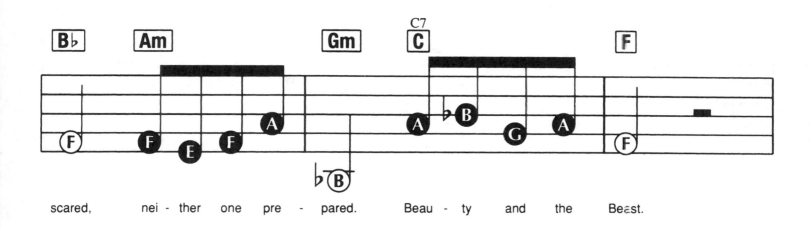

scared,   nei - ther one pre - pared.   Beau - ty and the Beast.

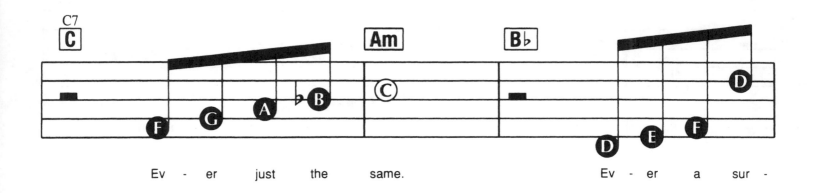

Ev - er just the same.   Ev - er a sur -

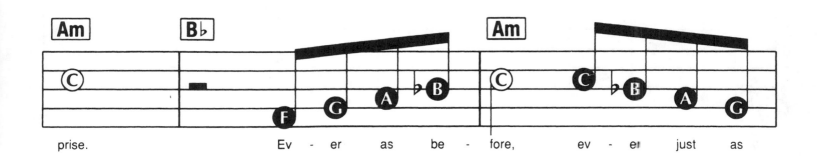

prise.   Ev - er as be - fore,   ev - er just as

4

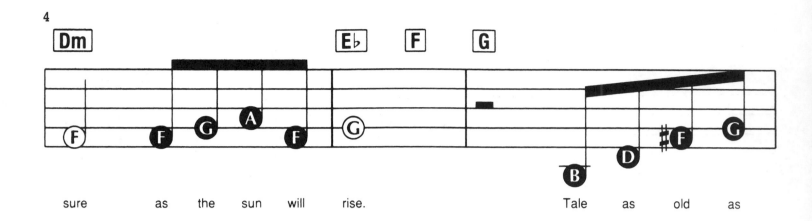

sure   as   the   sun   will   rise.   Tale   as   old   as

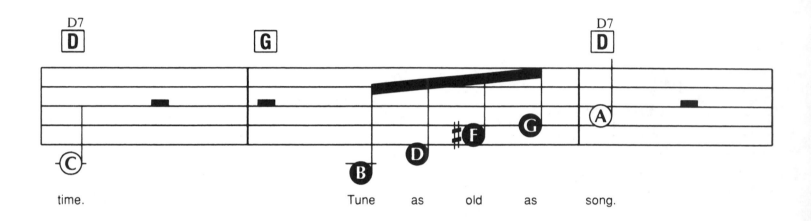

time.   Tune   as   old   as   song.

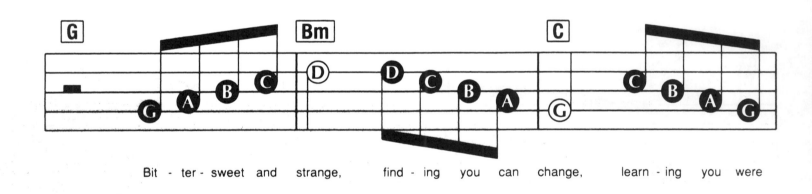

Bit - ter - sweet and   strange,   find - ing   you   can   change,   learn - ing   you   were

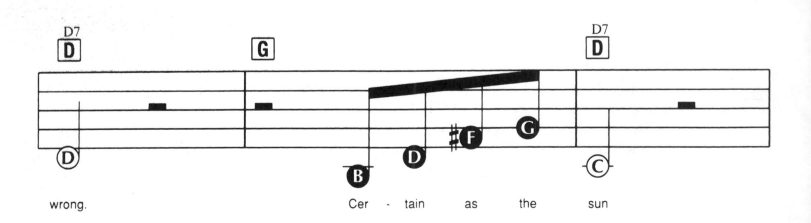

wrong.   Cer - tain   as   the   sun

5

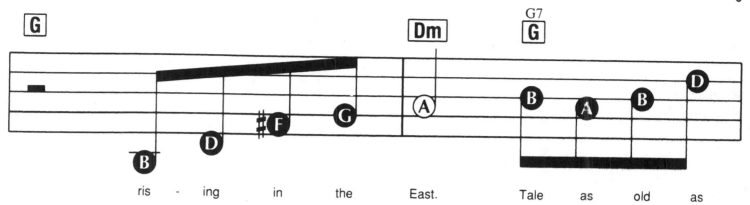

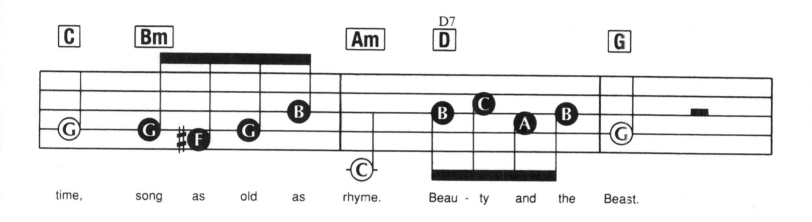

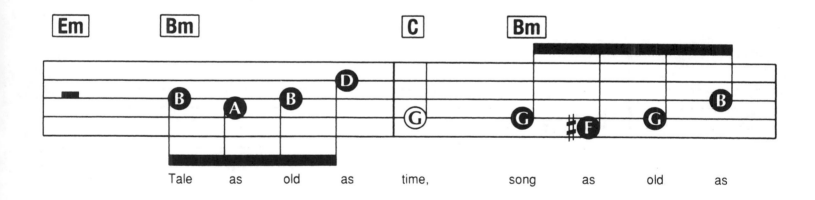

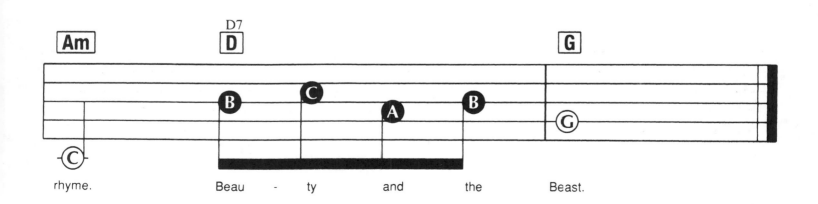

Bella notte
from LADY AND THE TRAMP

Registration 7
Rhythm: Fox Trot or Swing

Music and Lyrics by Peggy Lee
and Sonny Burke

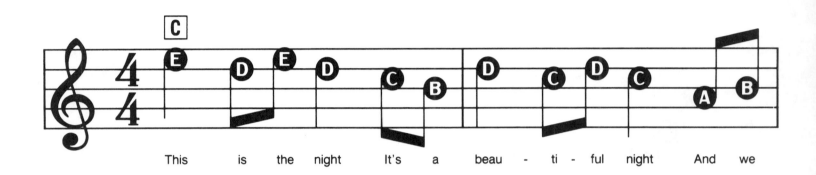

This is the night It's a beau - ti - ful night And we

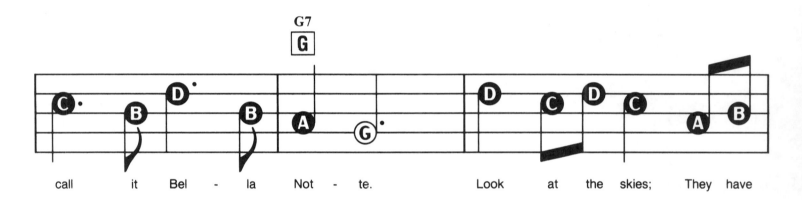

call it Bel - la Not - te. Look at the skies; They have

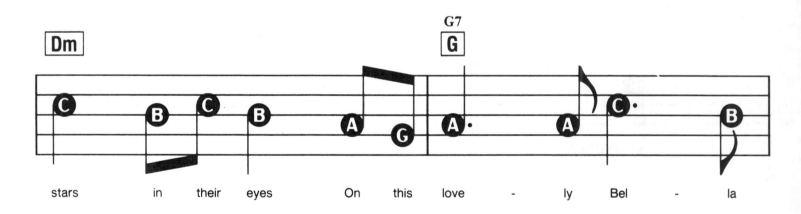

stars in their eyes On this love - ly Bel - la

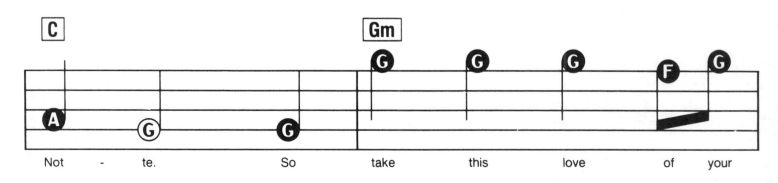

Not - te. So take this love of your

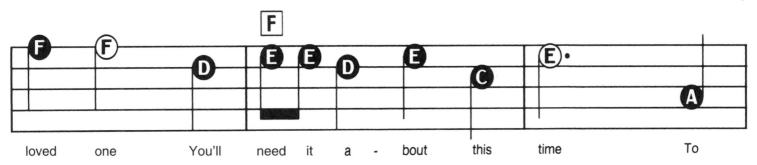

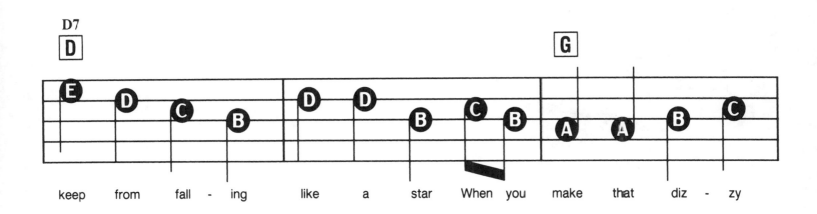

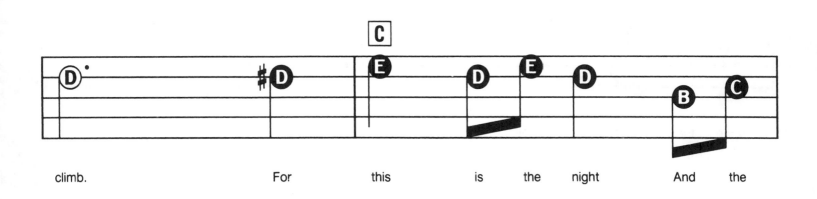

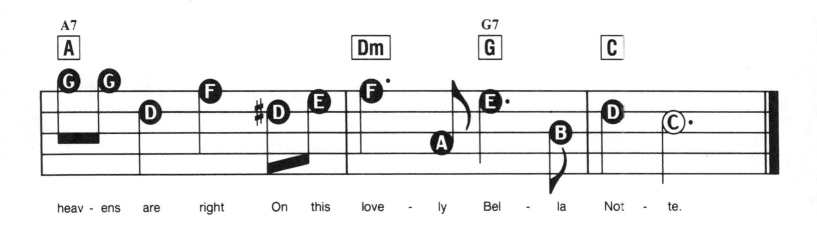

Can You Feel the Love Tonight
from THE LION KING

Registration 1
Rhythm: Ballad or Pops

Music by Elton John
Lyrics by Tim Rice

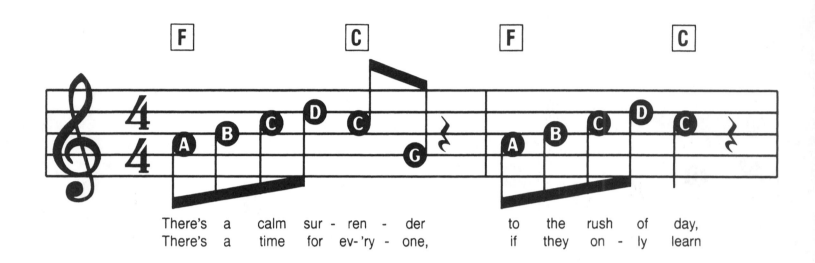

There's a calm sur-ren-der   to the rush of day,
There's a time for ev-'ry-one,   if they on-ly learn

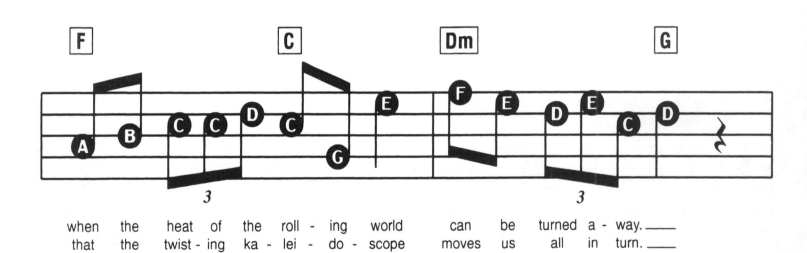

when the heat of the roll-ing world   can be turned a-way.____
that the twist-ing ka-lei-do-scope   moves us all in turn.____

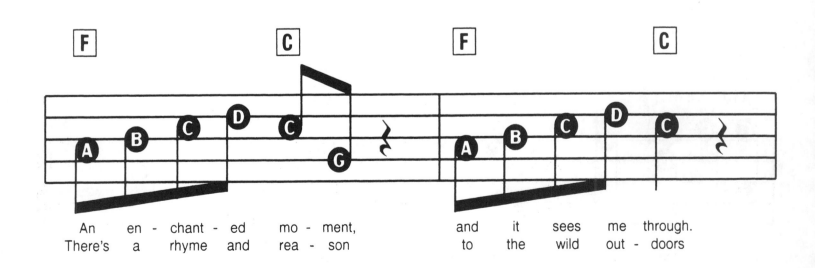

An en-chant-ed mo-ment,   and it sees me through.
There's a rhyme and rea-son   to the wild out-doors

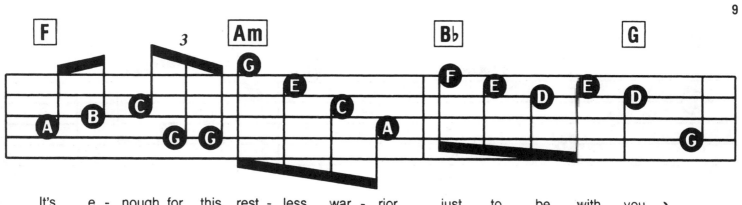

It's e - nough for this rest - less war - rior just to be with you.
when the heart of this star - crossed voy - ag - er beats in time with yours. } And

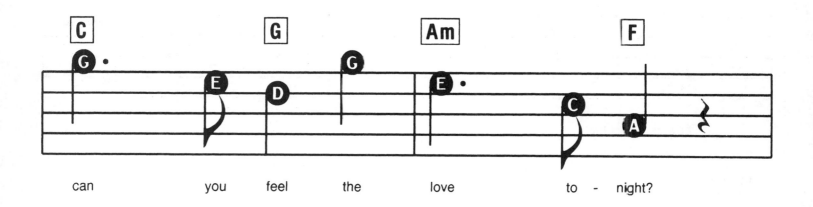

can you feel the love to - night?

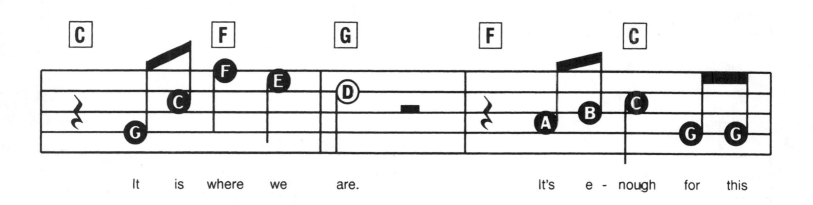

It is where we are. It's e - nough for this

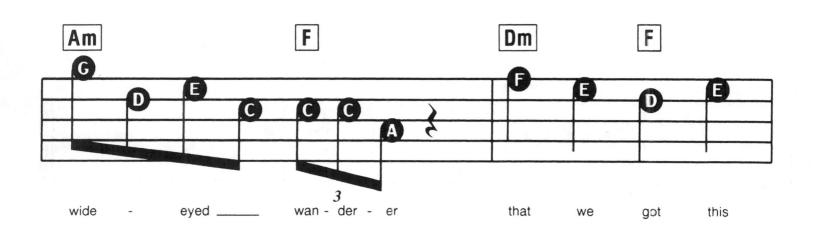

wide - eyed _____ wan - der - er that we got this

Candle on the Water
from PETE'S DRAGON

Registration 1
Rhythm: Ballad

Words and Music by Al Kasha
and Joel Hirschhom

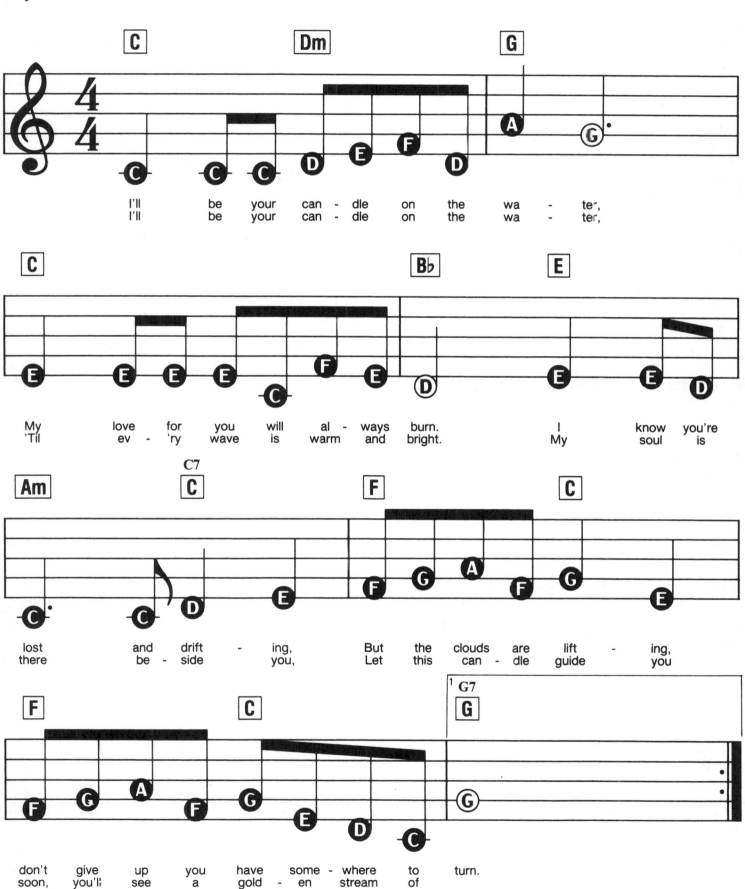

13

A Dream Is a Wish Your Heart Makes

from CINDERELLA

Registration 1
Rhythm: Ballad or Fox Trot

Words and Music by Mack David,
Al Hoffman and Jerry Livingston

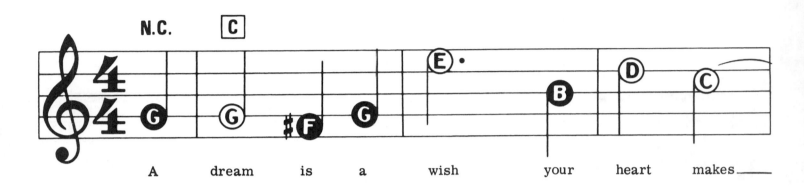

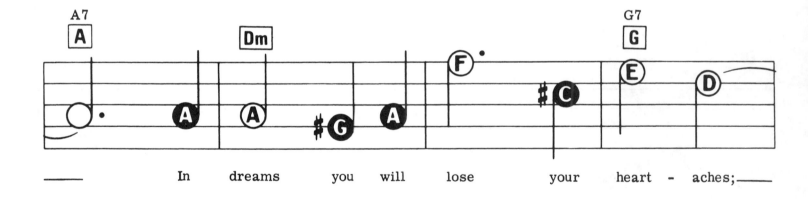

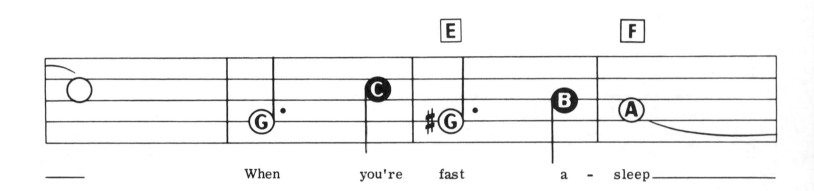

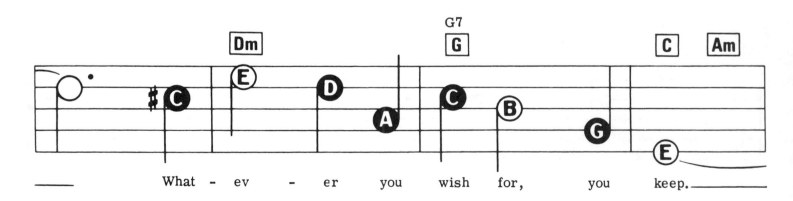

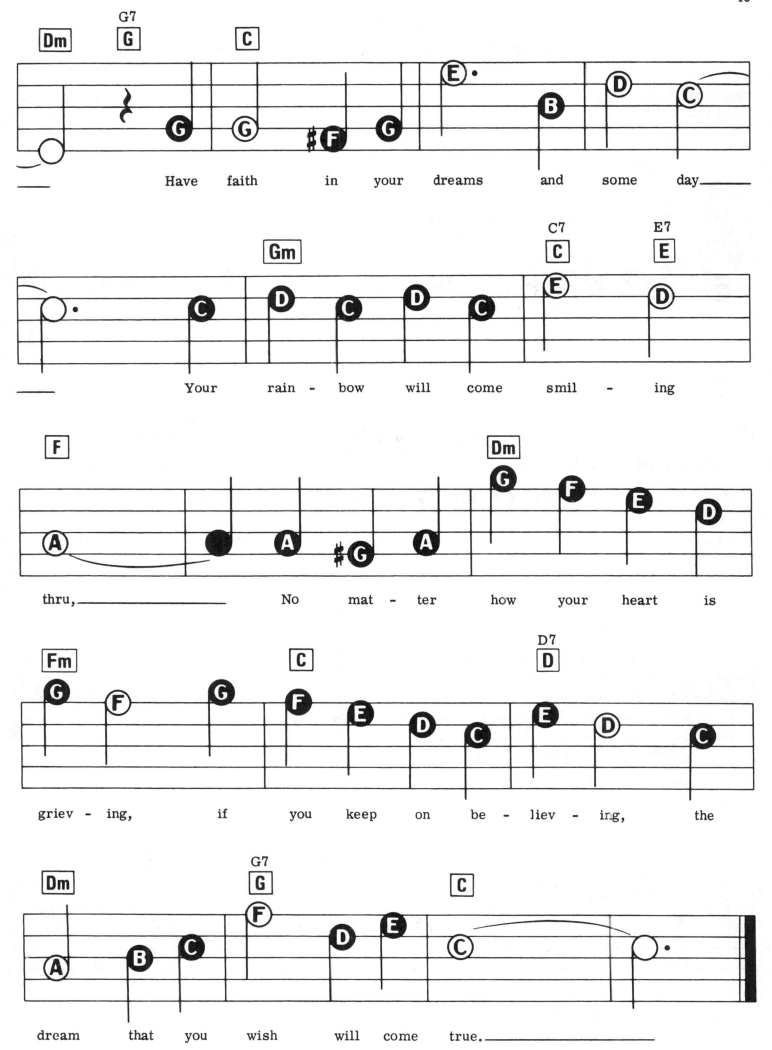

Evermore
from BEAUTY AND THE BEAST

Registration 2
Rhythm: Ballad

Music by Alan Menken
Lyrics by Tim Rice

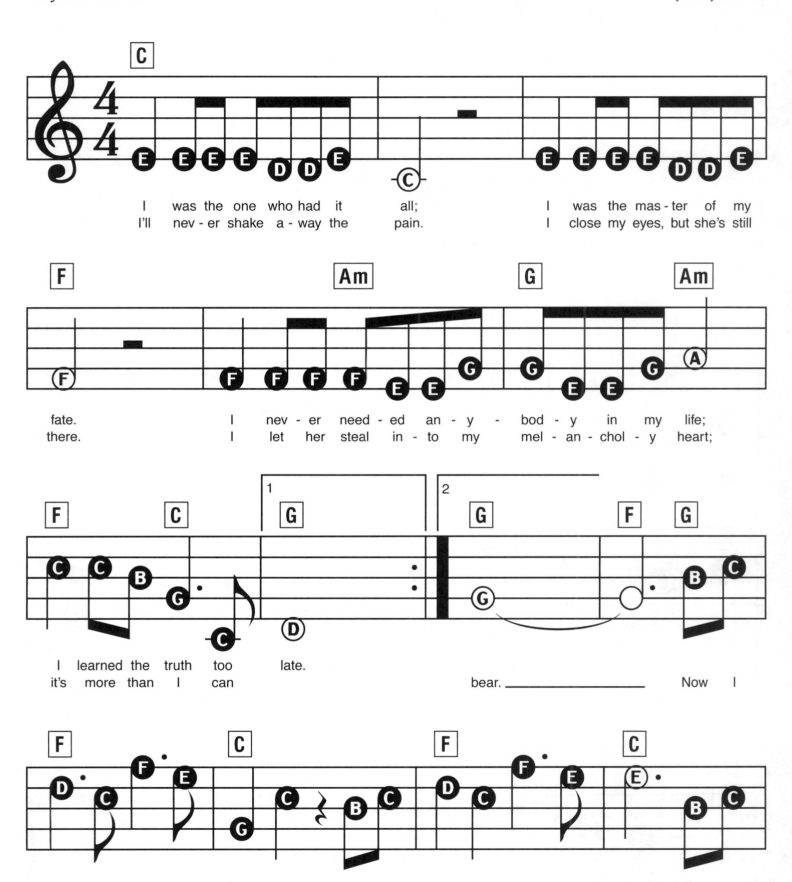

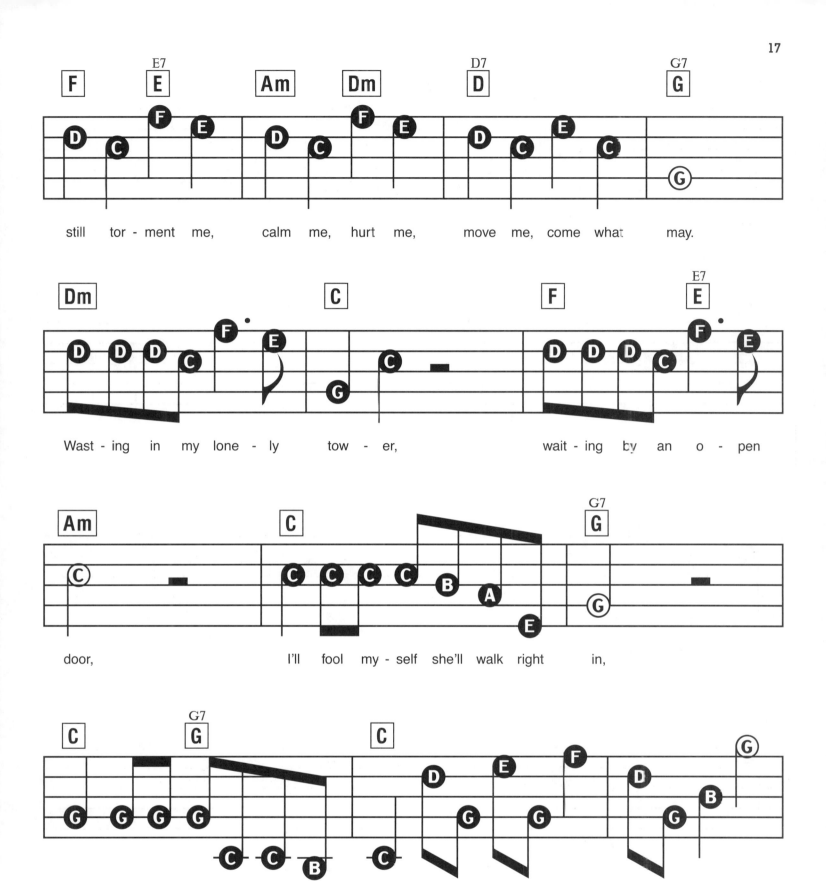

still tor - ment me, calm me, hurt me, move me, come what may.

Wast - ing in my lone - ly tow - er, wait - ing by an o - pen

door, I'll fool my - self she'll walk right in,

and be with me for - ev - er - more. *(Instrumental)*

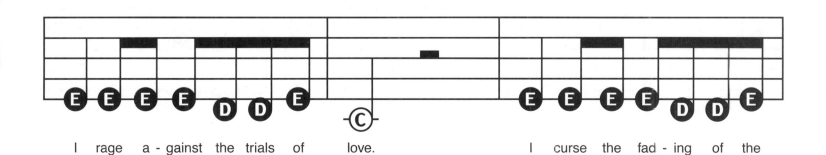

I rage a - gainst the trials of love. I curse the fad - ing of the

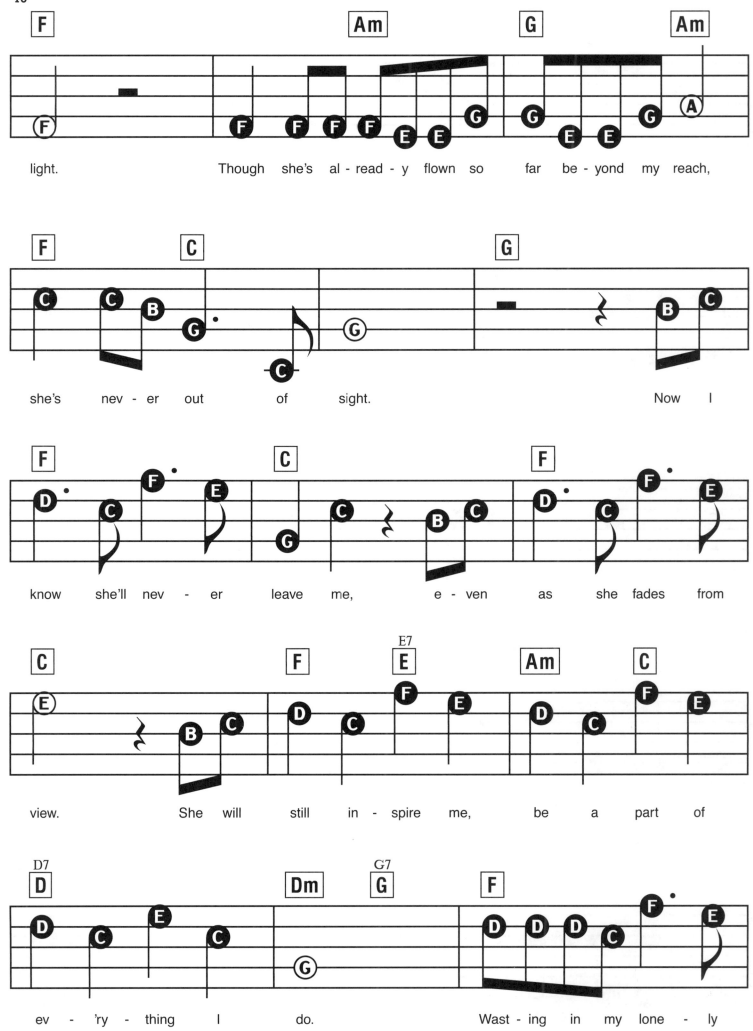

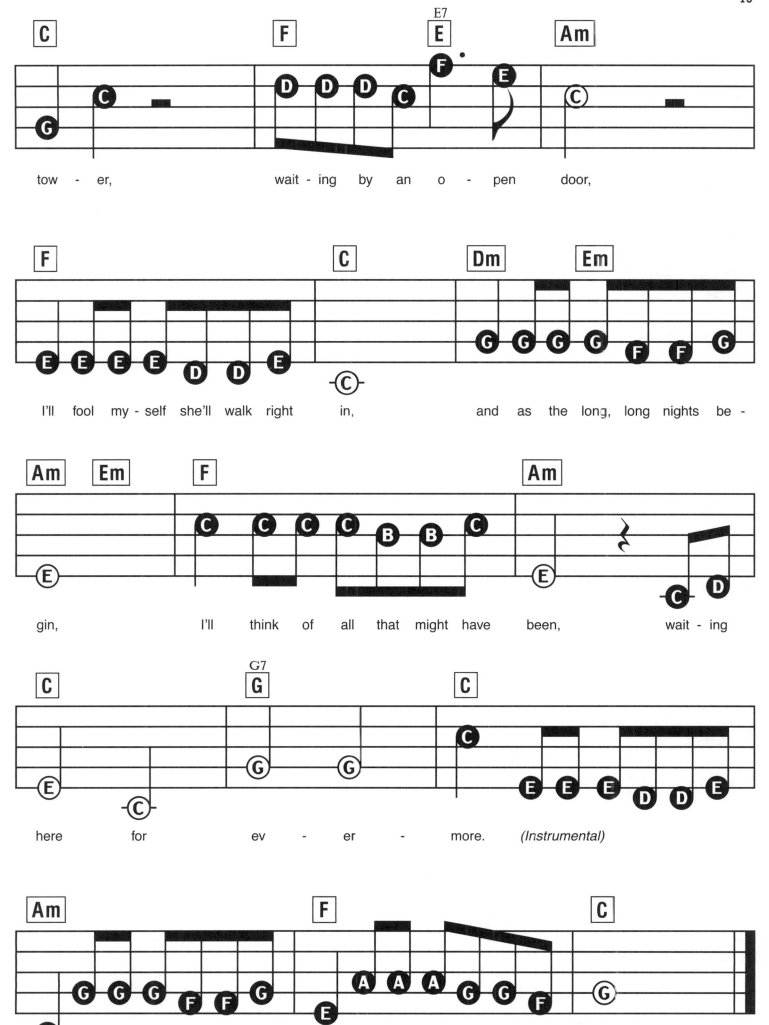

I See the Light
from TANGLED

Registration 4
Rhythm: Folk

Music by Alan Menken
Lyrics by Glenn Slater

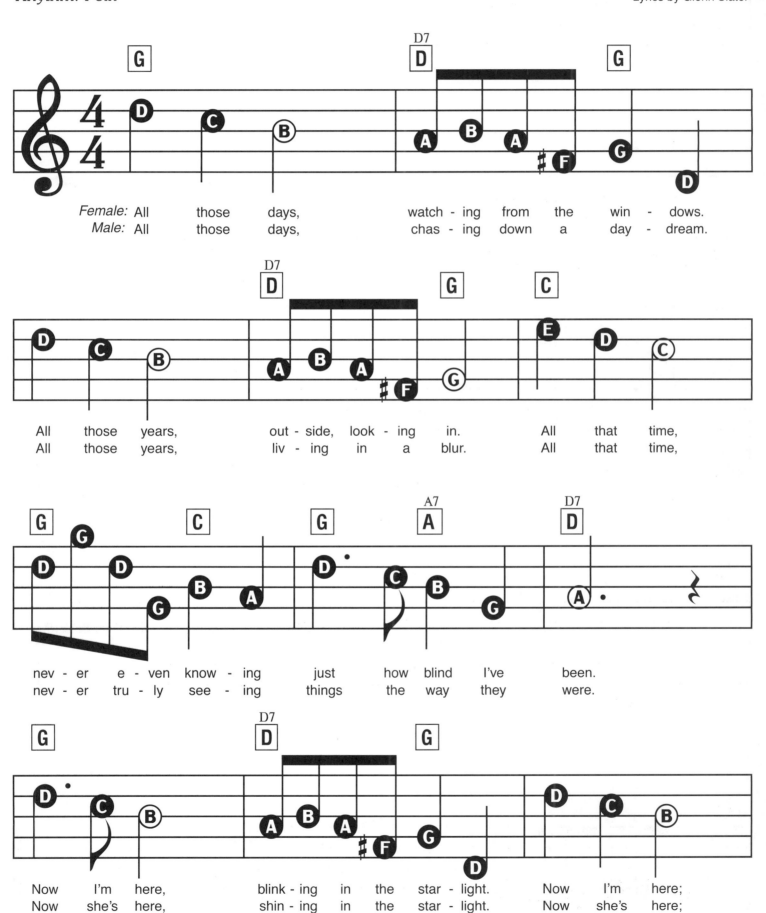

22

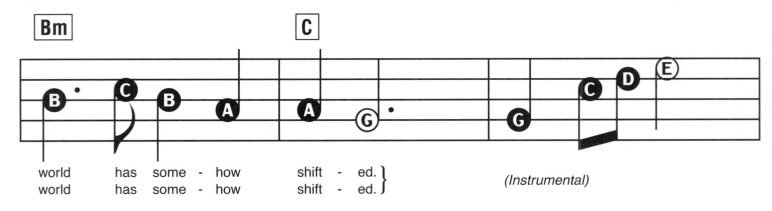

world has some - how shift - ed. }
world has some - how shift - ed. }

(Instrumental)

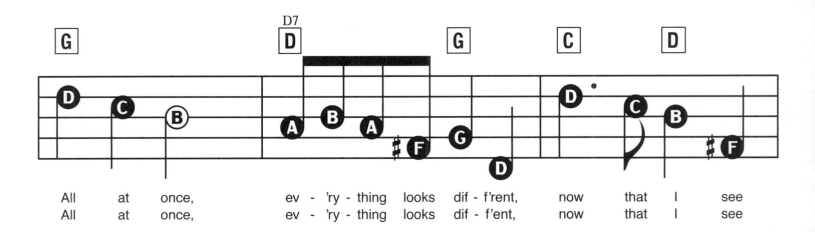

All at once, ev - 'ry - thing looks dif - f'rent, now that I see
All at once, ev - 'ry - thing looks dif - f'rent, now that I see

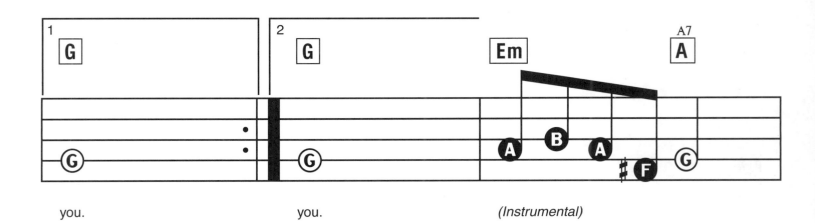

you.

you.

(Instrumental)

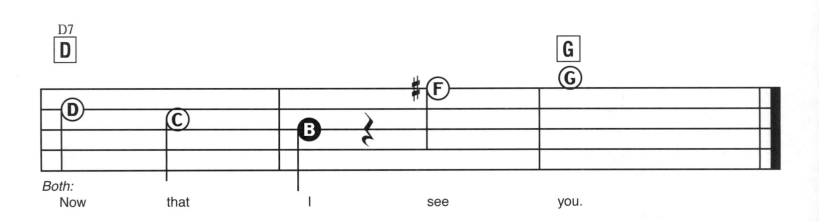

Both:
Now that I see you.

If I Never Knew You
(End Title)
from POCAHONTAS

Registration 3
Rhythm: Ballad or 8-Beat

Music by Alan Menken
Lyrics by Stephen Schwartz

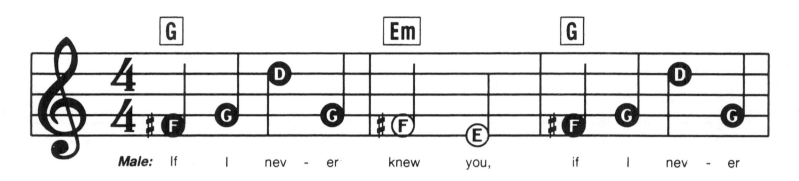

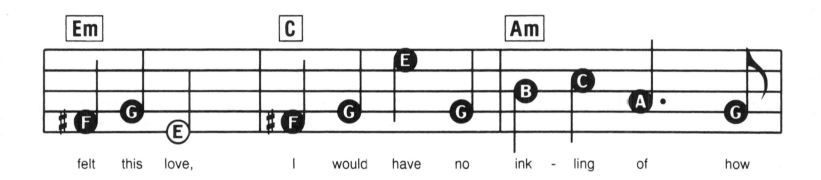

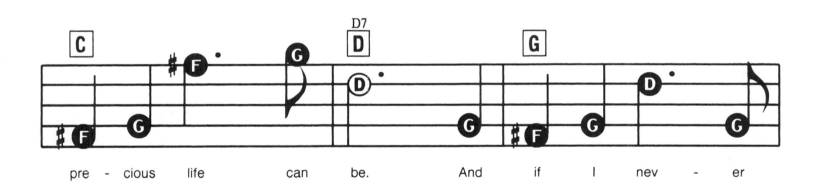

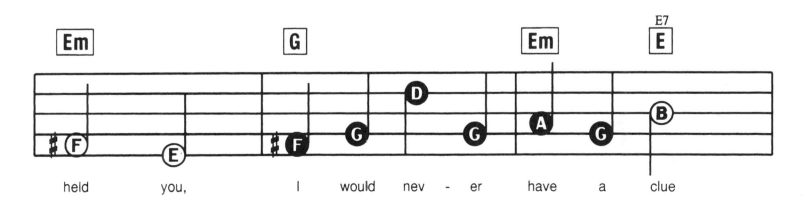

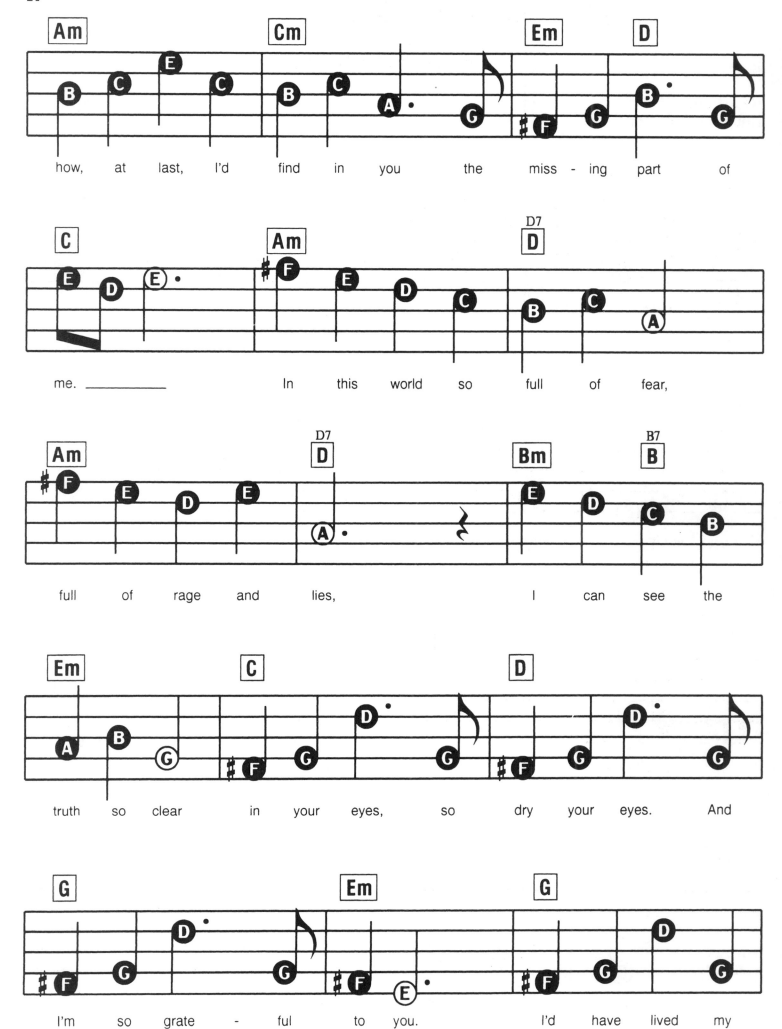

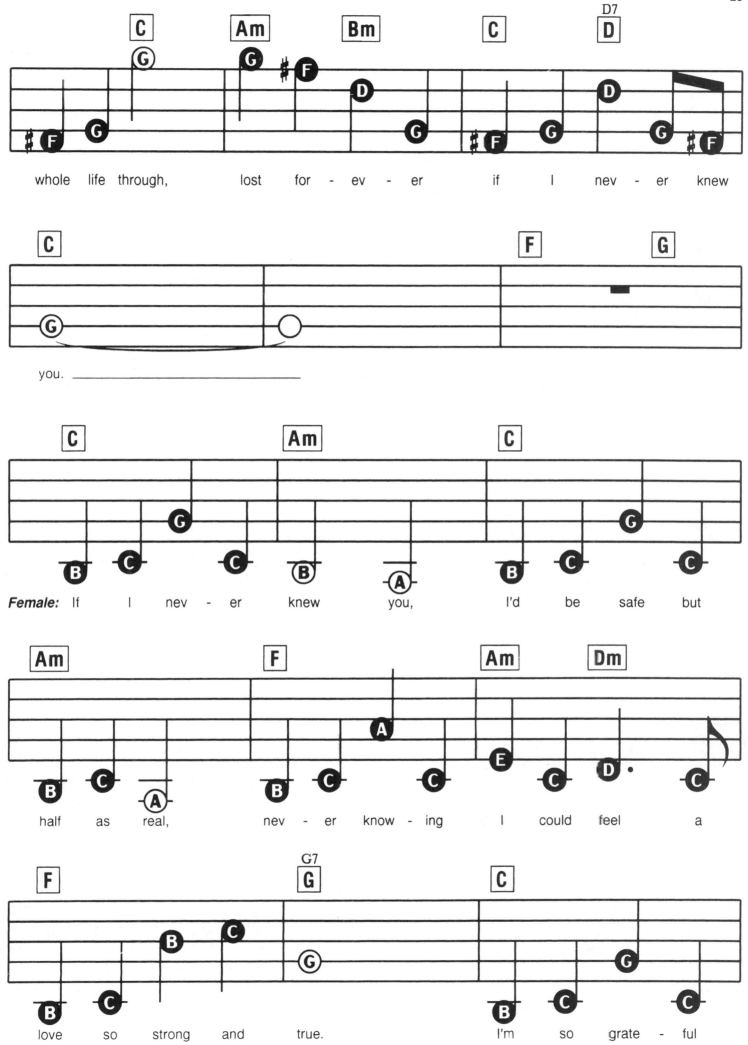

whole life through, lost for - ev - er if I nev - er knew

you. _____

Female: If I nev - er knew you, I'd be safe but

half as real, nev - er know - ing I could feel a

love so strong and true. I'm so grate - ful

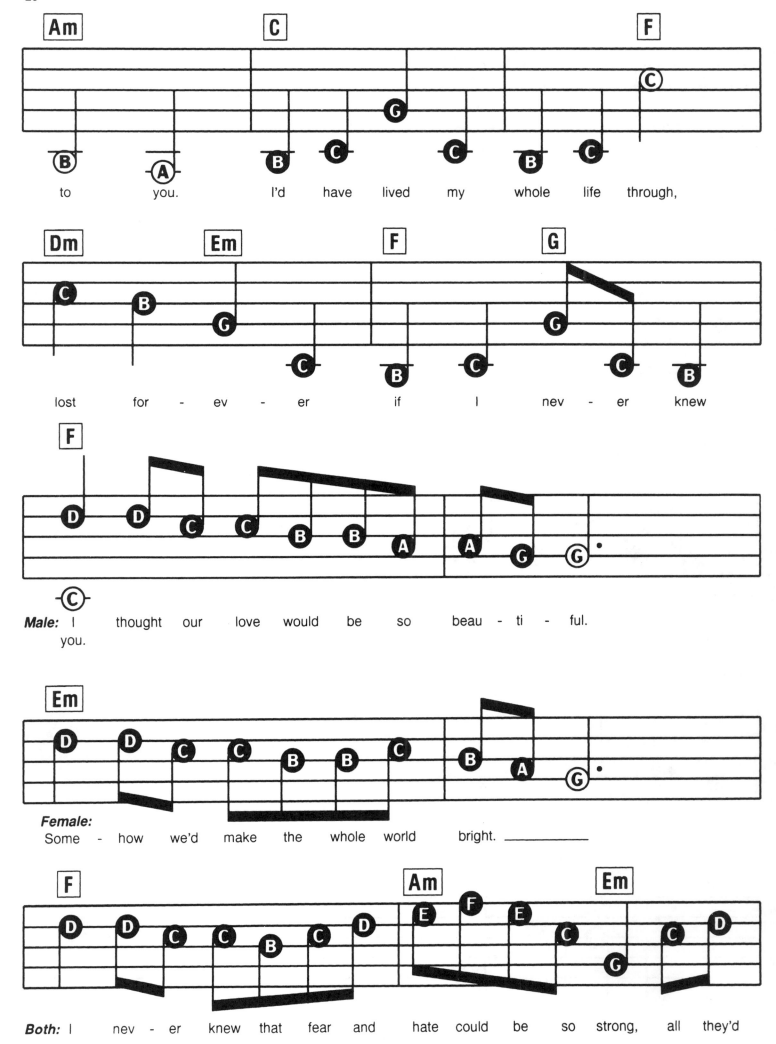

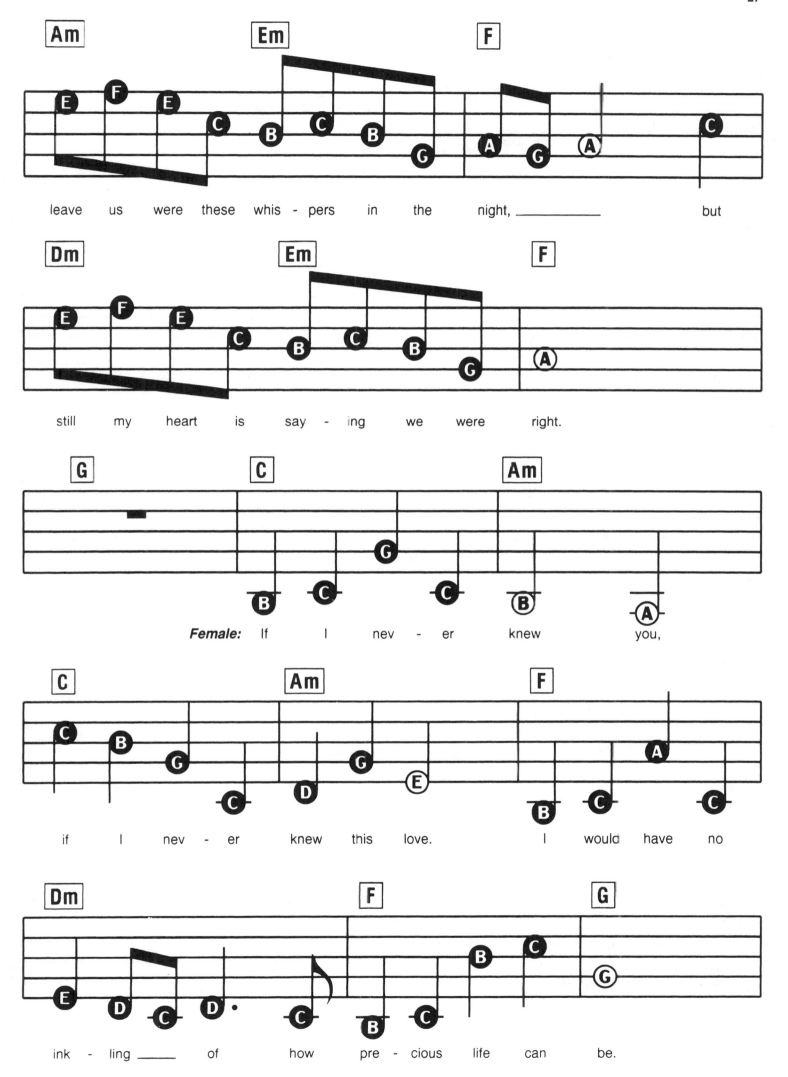

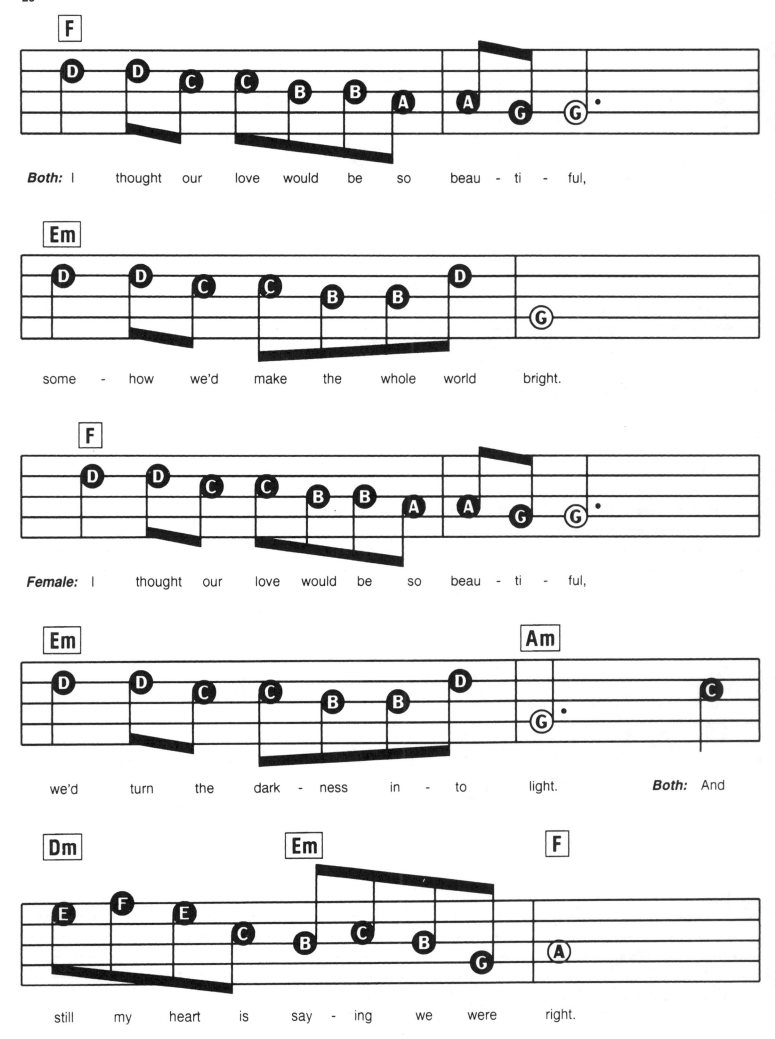

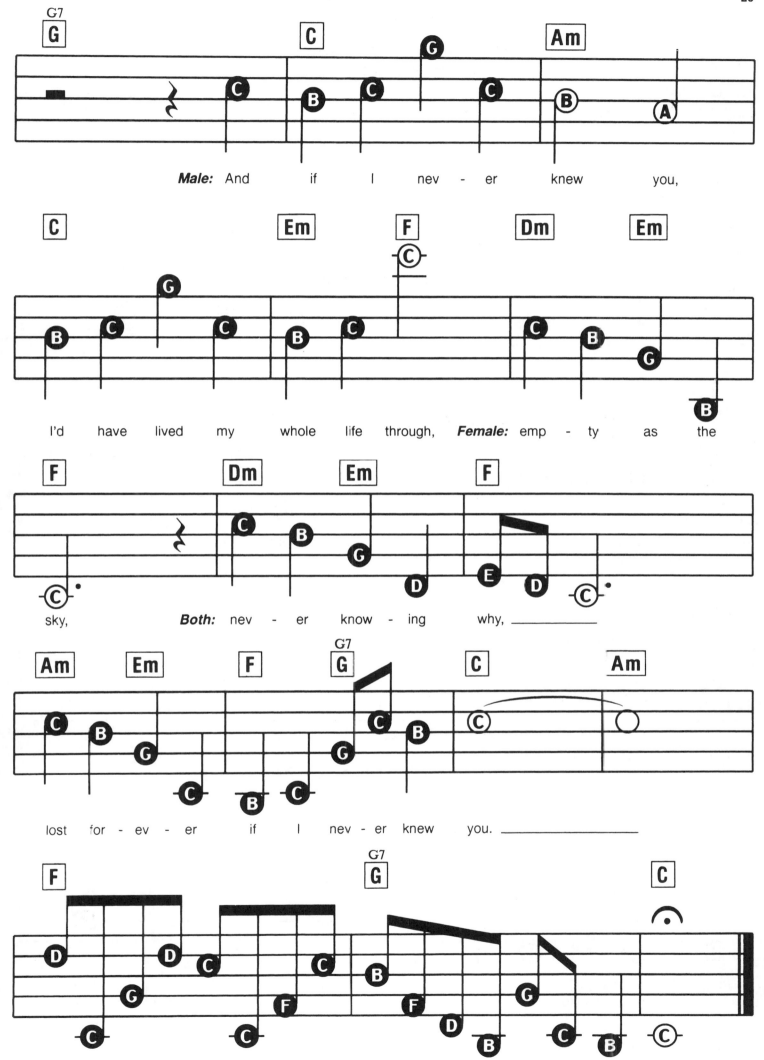

I Won't Say
(I'm in Love)
from HERCULES

Registration 1
Rhythm: Pop or 8-Beat

Music by Alan Menken
Lyrics by David Zippel

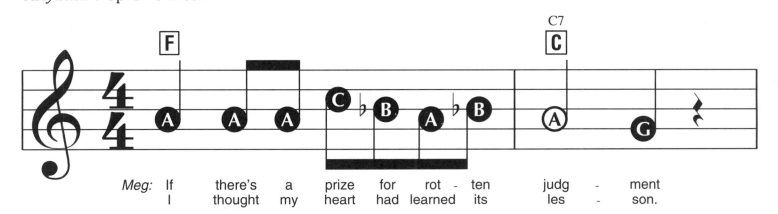

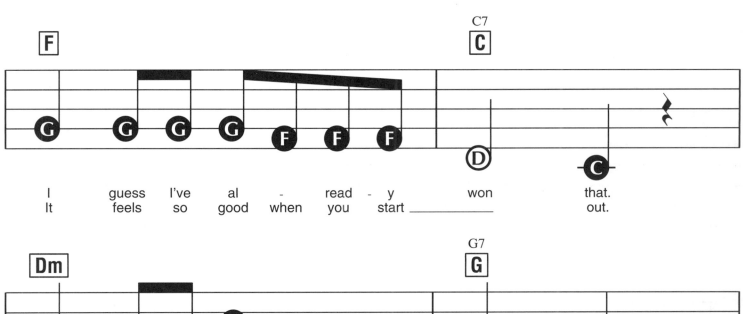

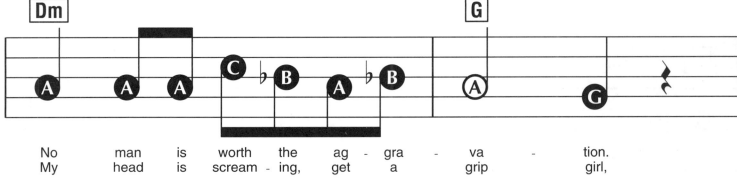

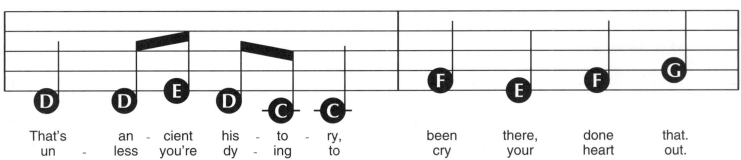

32

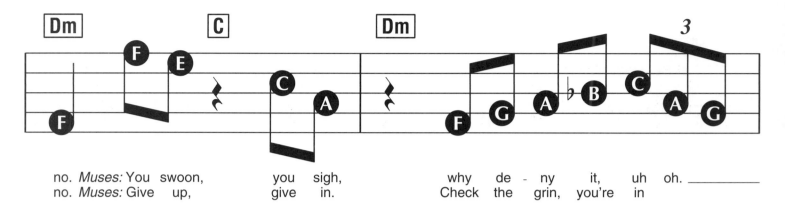

no. *Muses:* You swoon, you sigh, why de - ny it, uh oh. _____
no. *Muses:* Give up, give in. Check the grin, you're in

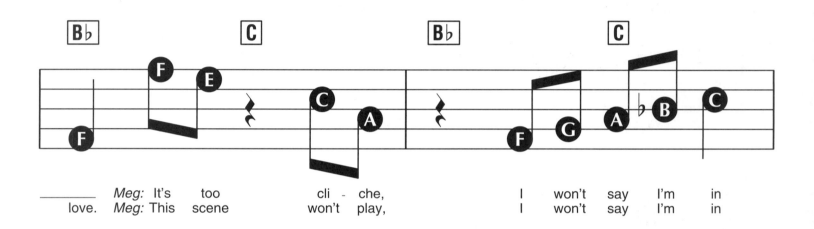

_____ *Meg:* It's too cli - che, I won't say I'm in
love. *Meg:* This scene won't play, I won't say I'm in

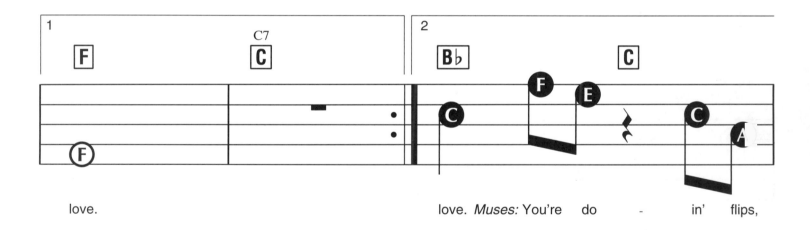

love.

love. *Muses:* You're do - in' flips,

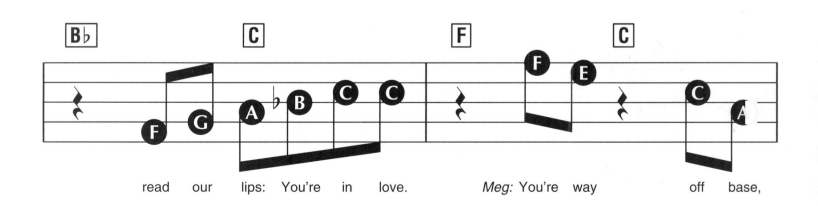

read our lips: You're in love. *Meg:* You're way off base,

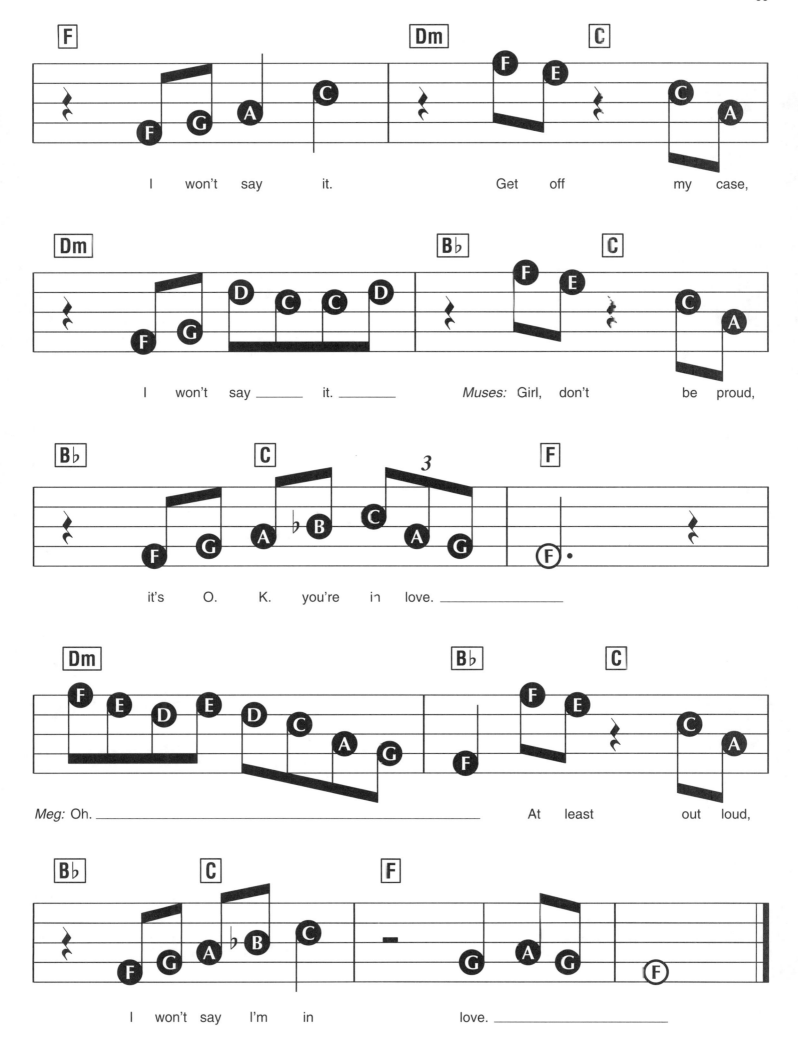

Kiss the Girl
from THE LITTLE MERMAID

Registration 7
Rhythm: Bossa Nova or Latin

Music by Alan Menken
Lyrics by Howard Ashman

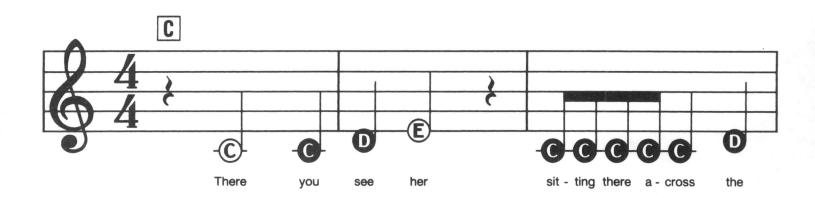

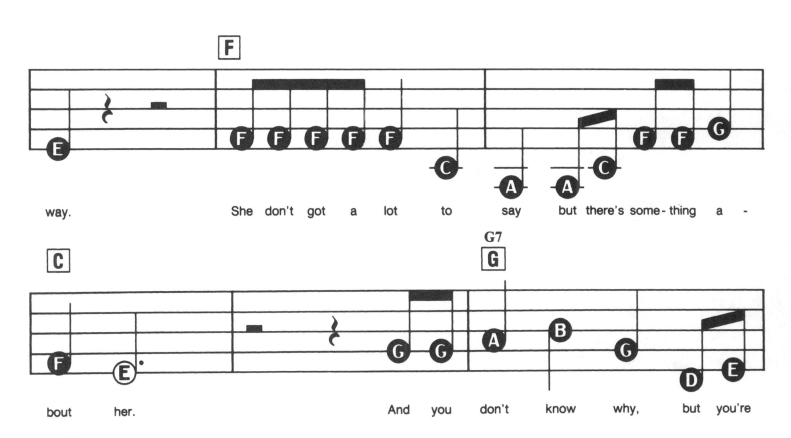

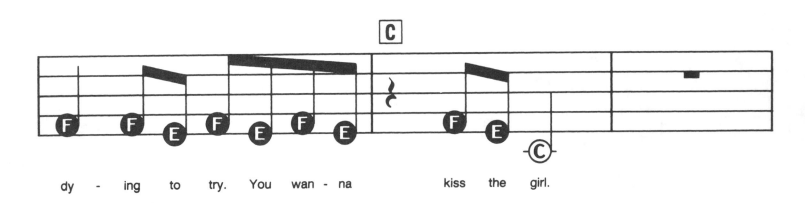

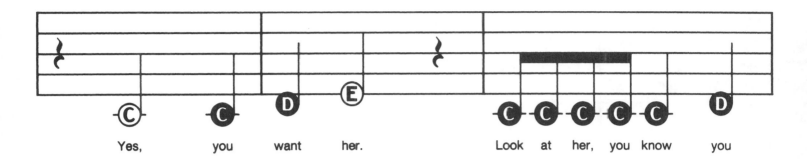

Yes, you want her. Look at her, you know you

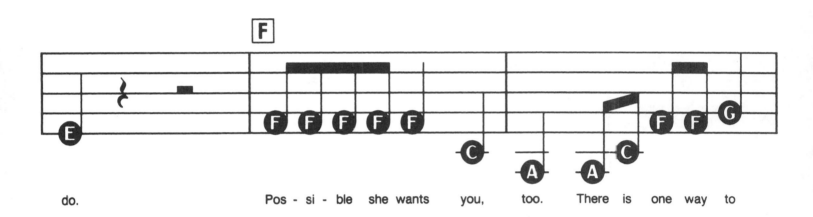

do. Pos - si - ble she wants you, too. There is one way to

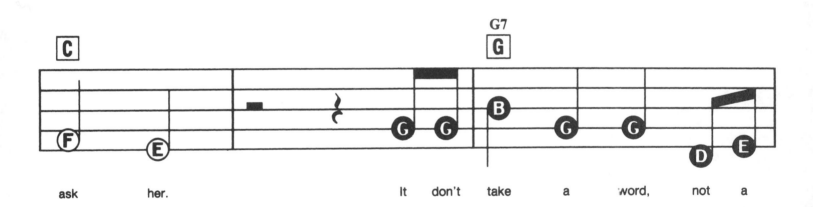

ask her. It don't take a word, not a

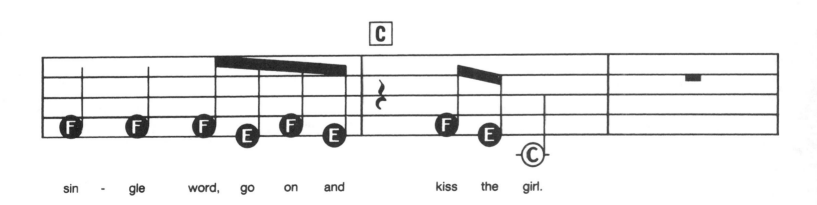

sin - gle word, go on and kiss the girl.

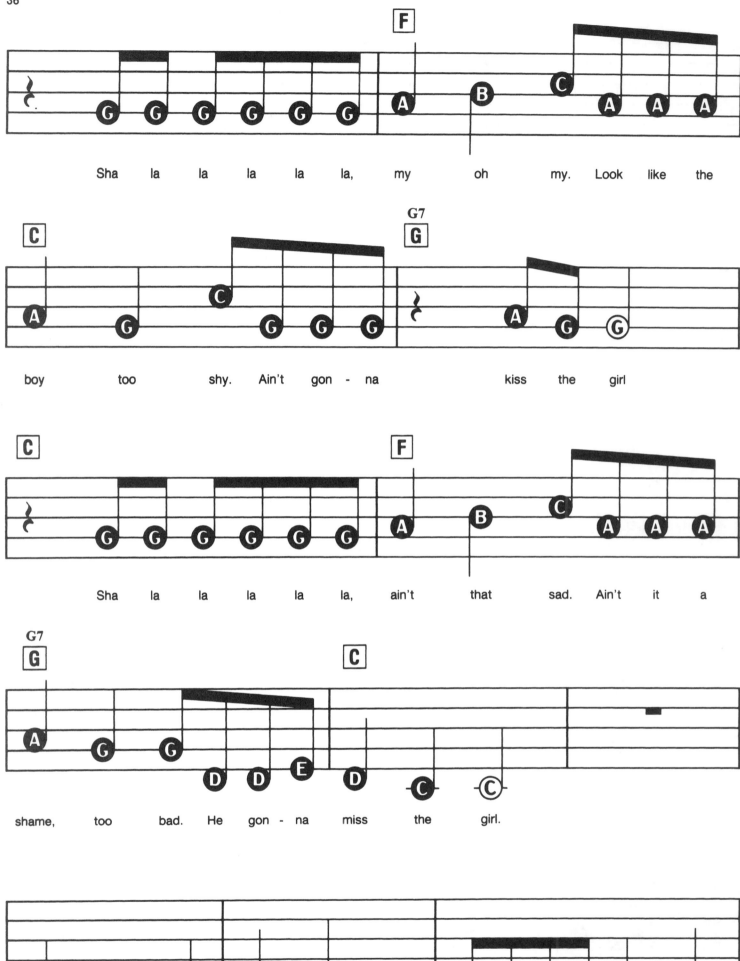

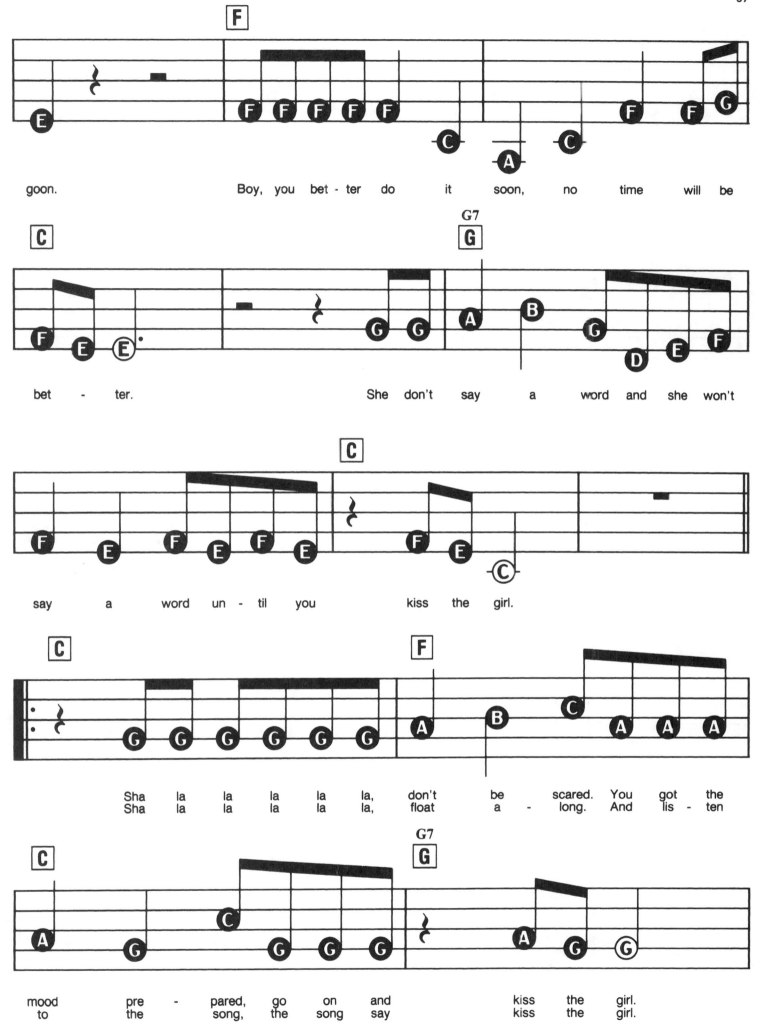

Love Is an Open Door
from FROZEN

Registration 1
Rhythm: 8-Beat or Rock

Music and Lyrics by Kristen Anderson-Lopez
and Robert Lopez

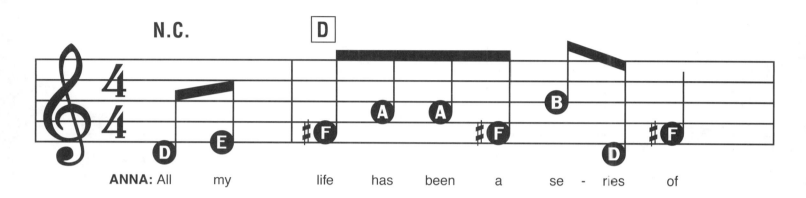

ANNA: All my life has been a se - ries of

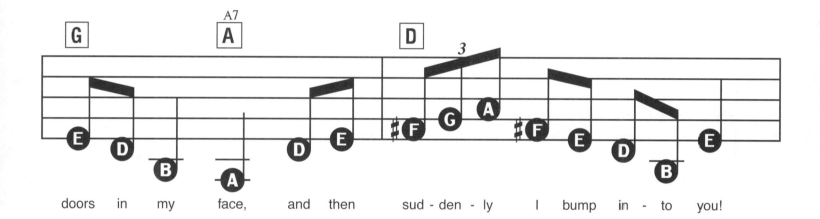

doors in my face, and then sud - den - ly I bump in - to you!

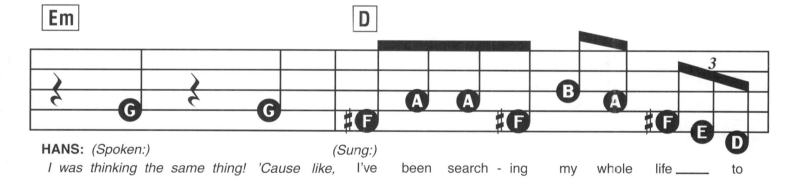

HANS: (Spoken:)   (Sung:)
I was thinking the same thing! 'Cause like, I've been search - ing my whole life _____ to

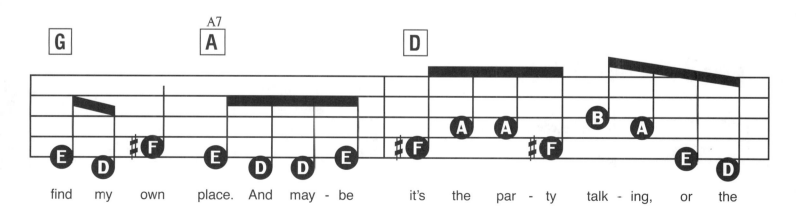

find my own place. And may - be it's the par - ty talk - ing, or the

40

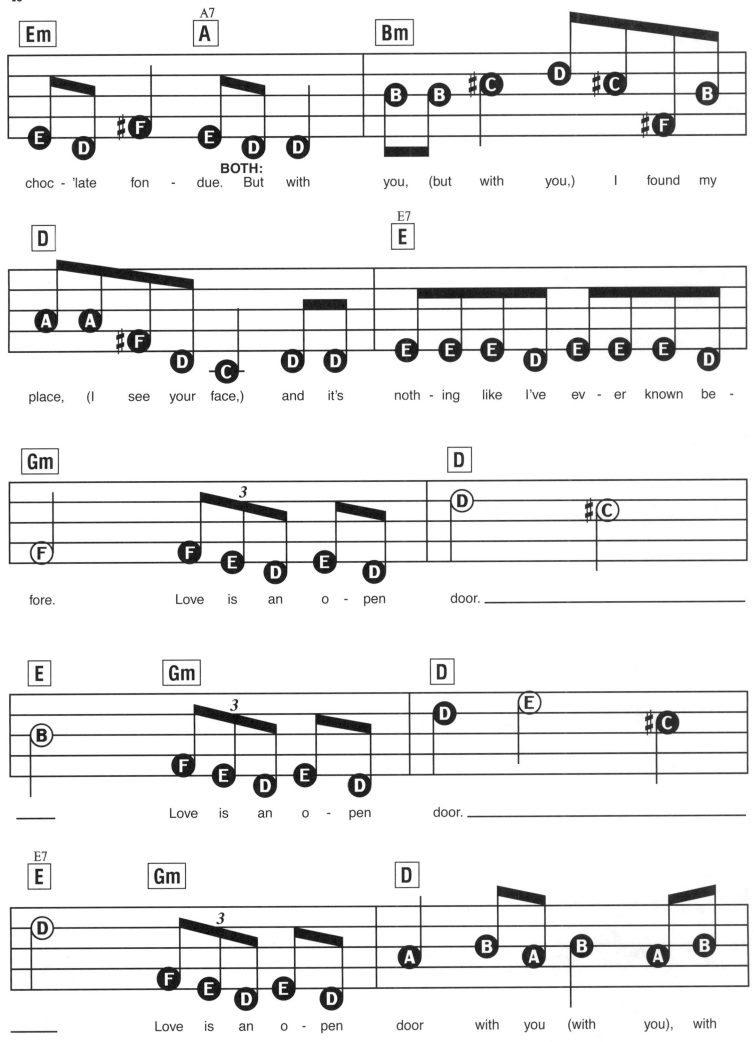

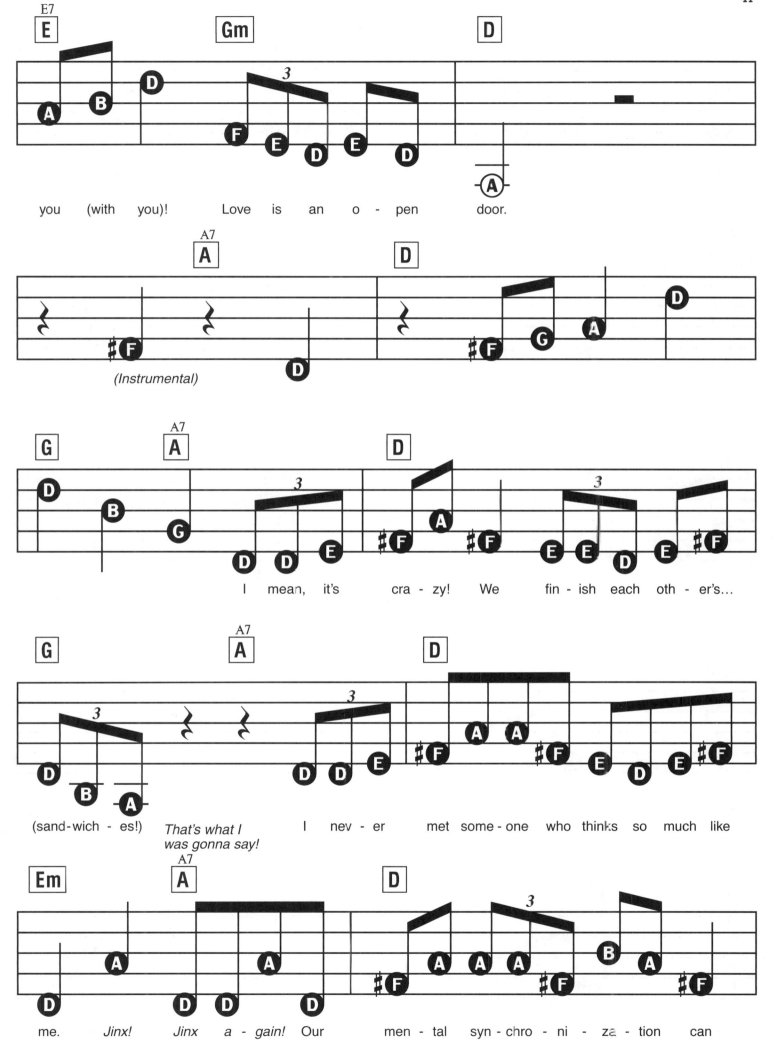

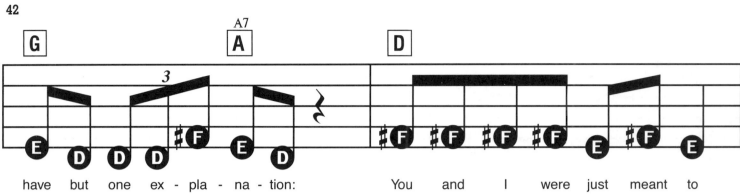

have but one ex - pla - na - tion: You and I were just meant to

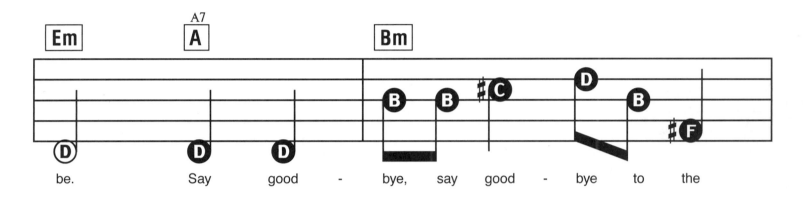

be. Say good - bye, say good - bye to the

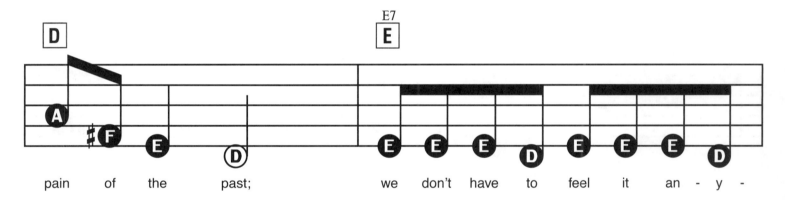

pain of the past; we don't have to feel it an - y -

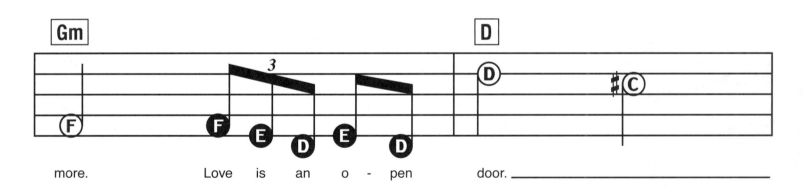

more. Love is an o - pen door. _____

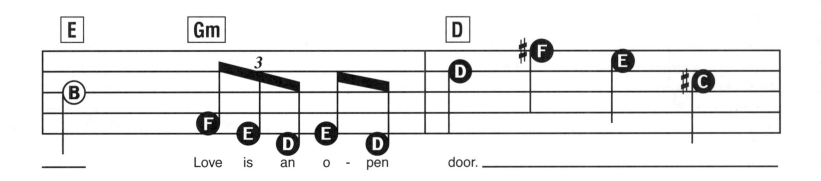

_____ Love is an o - pen door. _____

43

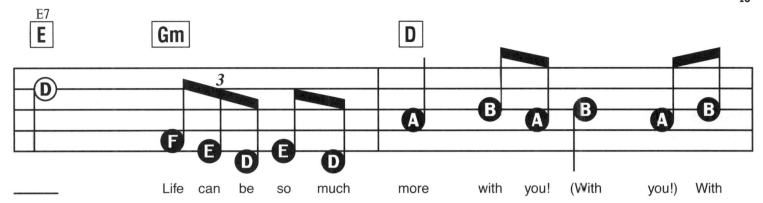

_____ Life can be so much more with you! (With you!) With

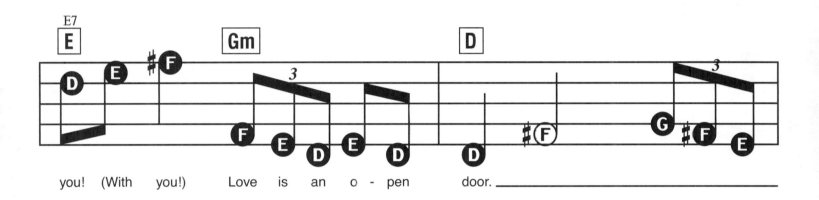

you! (With you!) Love is an o - pen door. _____

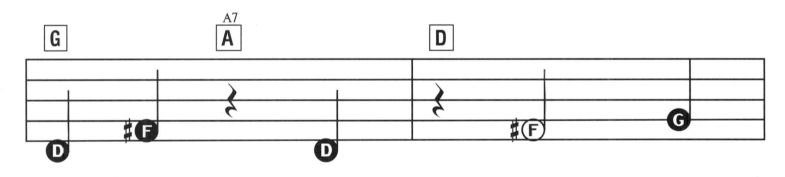

_____

HANS: *(Spoken:) Can I say something crazy? Will you marry me?*

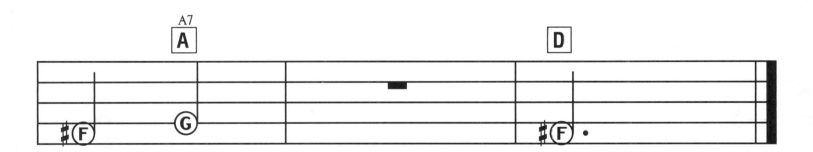

ANNA: *Can I say something even crazier? Yes!*

Love
from ROBIN HOOD

Registration 2
Rhythm: Fox Trot or Swing

Words by Floyd Huddleston
Music by George Bruns

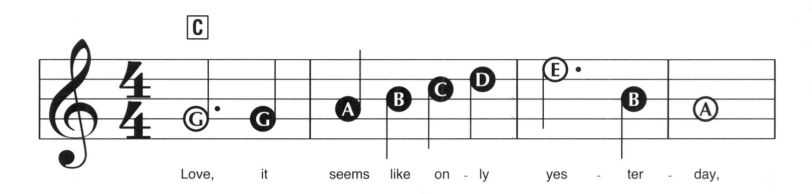

Love, it seems like on - ly yes - ter - day,

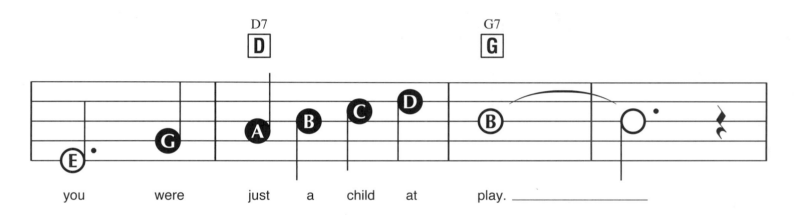

you were just a child at play. _____

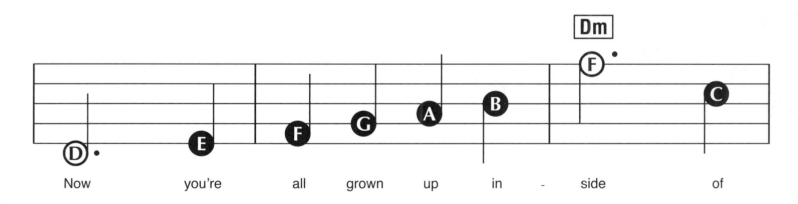

Now you're all grown up in - side of

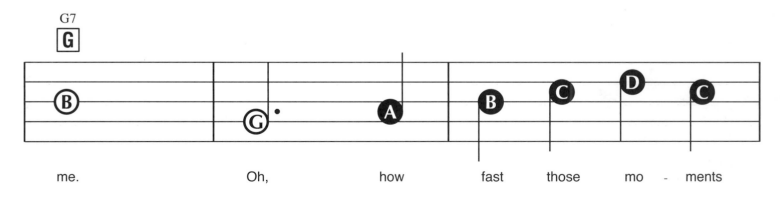

me. Oh, how fast those mo - ments

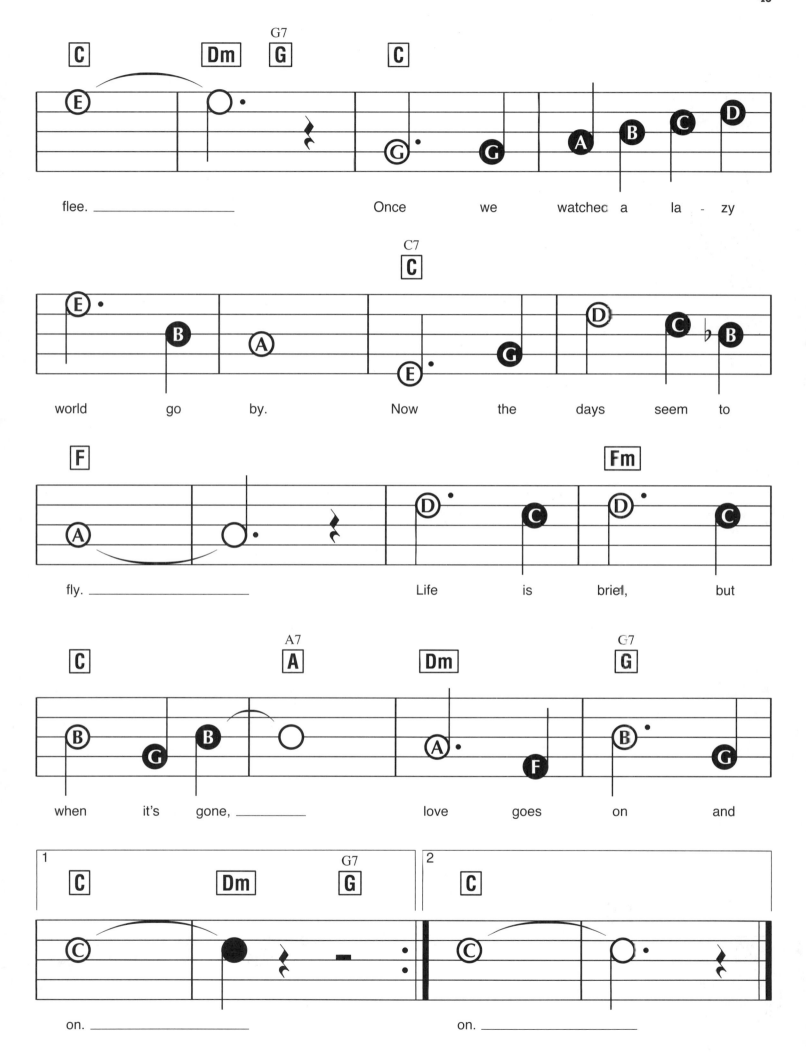

Once Upon a Dream
from SLEEPING BEAUTY

Registration 2
Rhythm: Waltz

Words and Music by Sammy Fain
and Jack Lawrence
Adapted from a Theme by Tchaikovsky

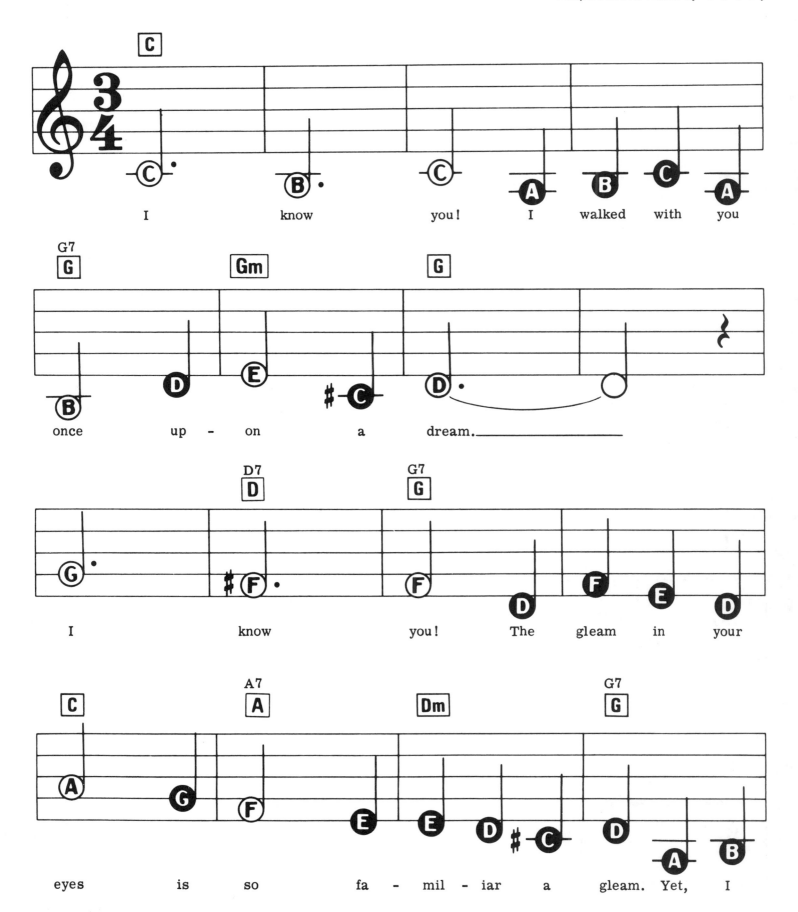

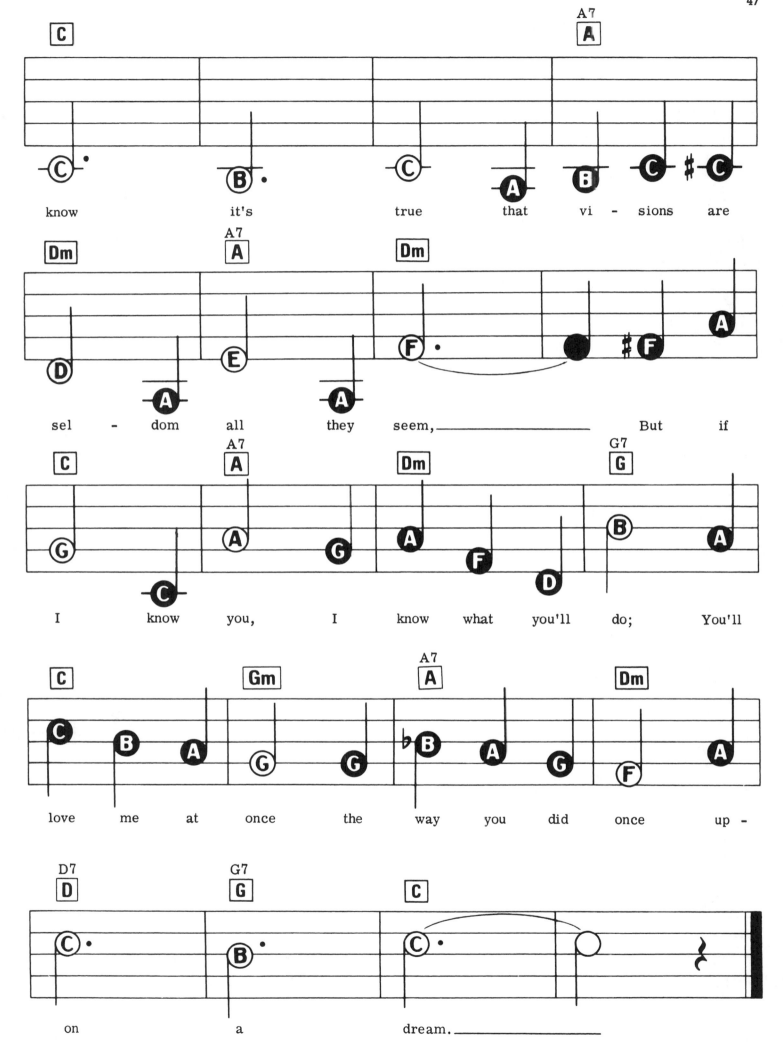

So Dear to My Heart
from SO DEAR TO MY HEART

Registration 10
Rhythm: Fox Trot or Swing

Words by Irving Taylor
Music by Ticker Freeman

N.C.
C B D B
So dear to my

F
C F G A ♭B ♯G
heart that Sep - tem - ber - y
heart that Sep - tem - ber - y

A A C G G C F D
day with the leaves turn - ing brown and
day when that old sha - dy lane we

C7 / C
E ♯C
gold when
strolled was

Gm
D D D C D C
you were the dream I would
just turn - ing scar - let and

D7 / D

Gm
♭B
hold
gold

C7 / C
A G F E
so dear to my
so dear to my

F
C
heart. _____

C7 / C
(held note)
heart. _____

C B D B
So dear to my
So dear to my

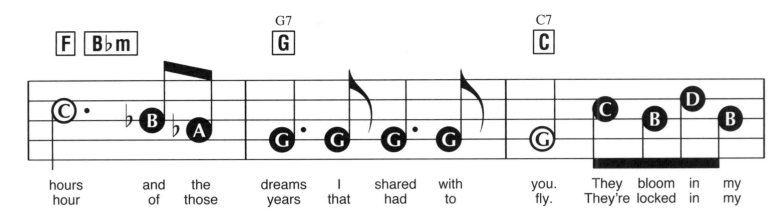

hours and the dreams I shared with you. They bloom in my
hour of those years that had to fly. They're locked in my

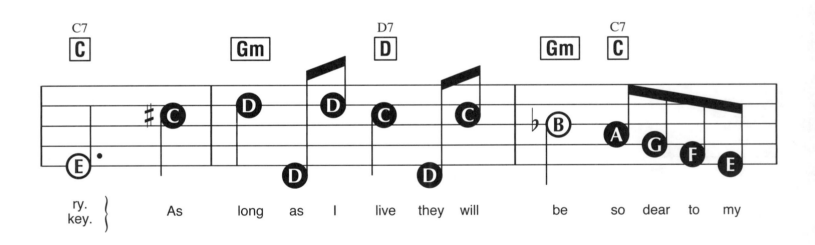

heart in a cor - ner a - part ev - 'ry sweet ten - der mem - o -
heart in a cor - ner a - part while I ten - der - ly hold the

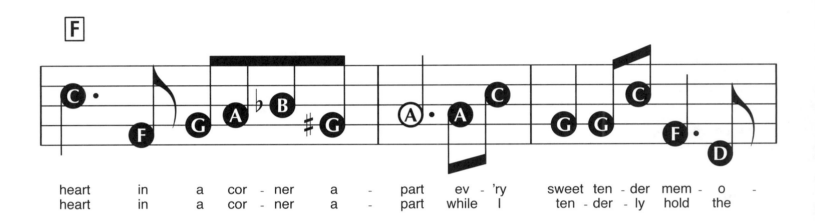

ry. } As long as I live they will be so dear to my
key. }

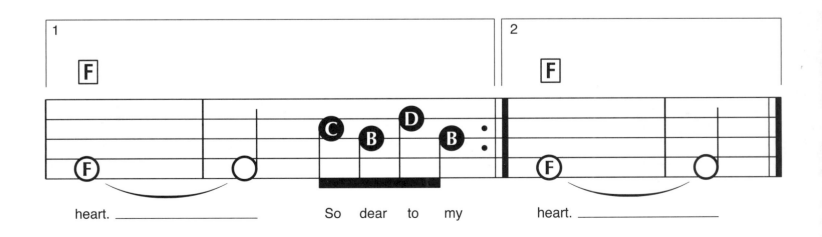

heart. _____ So dear to my heart. _____

A Whole New World
(Aladdin's Theme)
from ALADDIN

Registration 1
Rhythm: Pops

Music by Alan Menken
Lyrics by Tim Rice

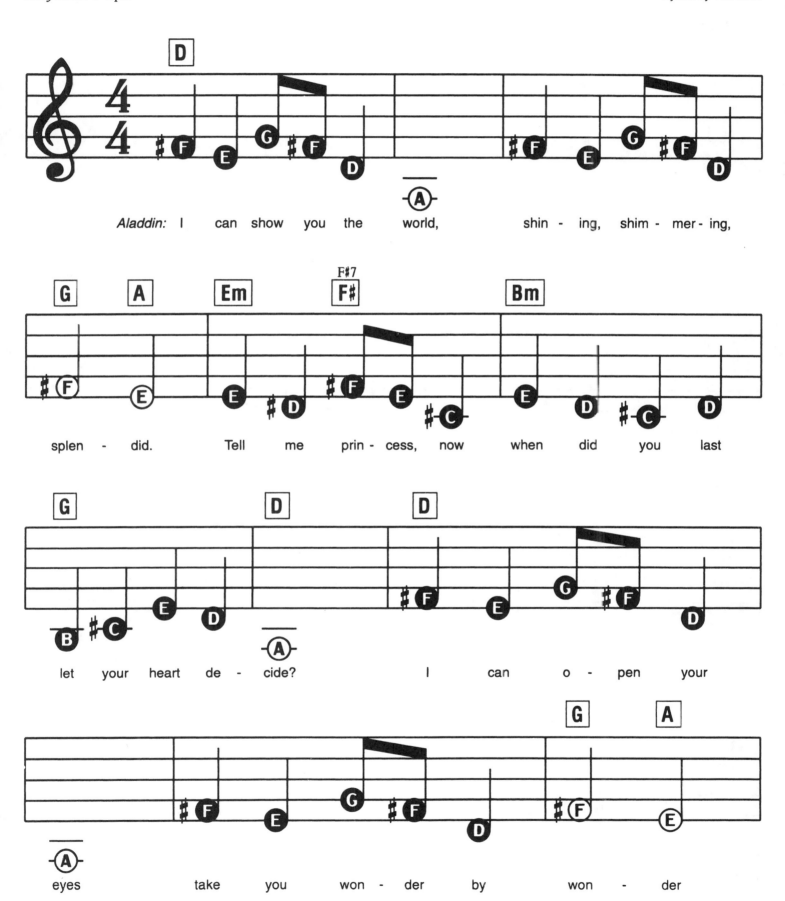

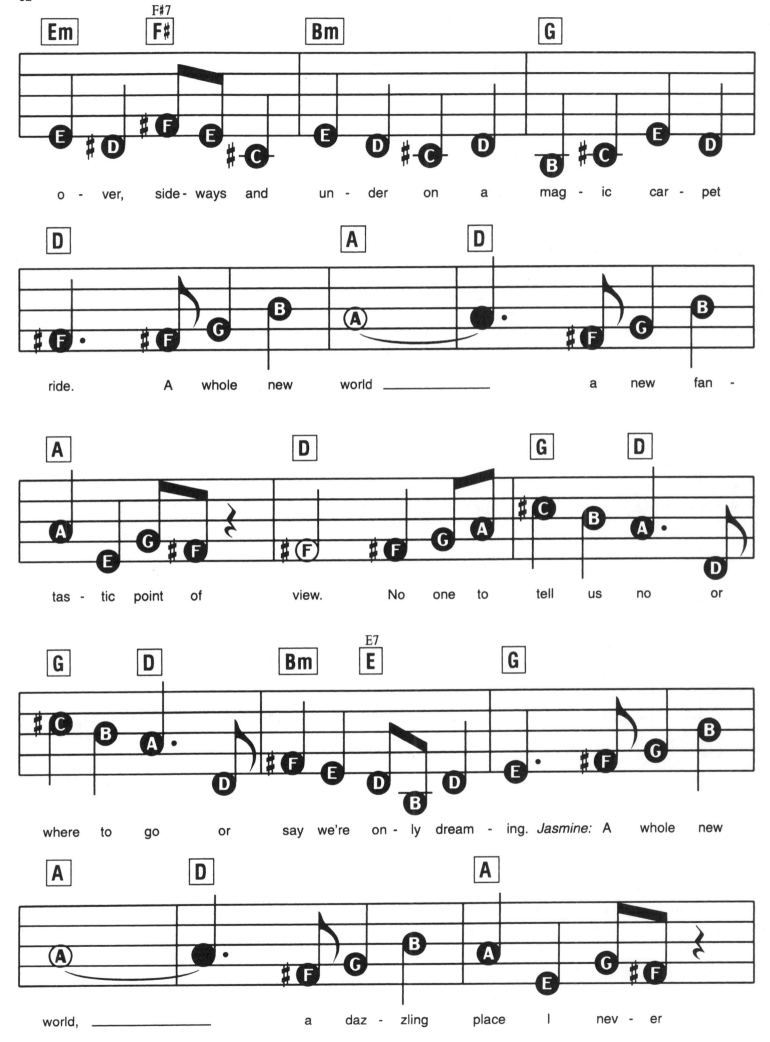

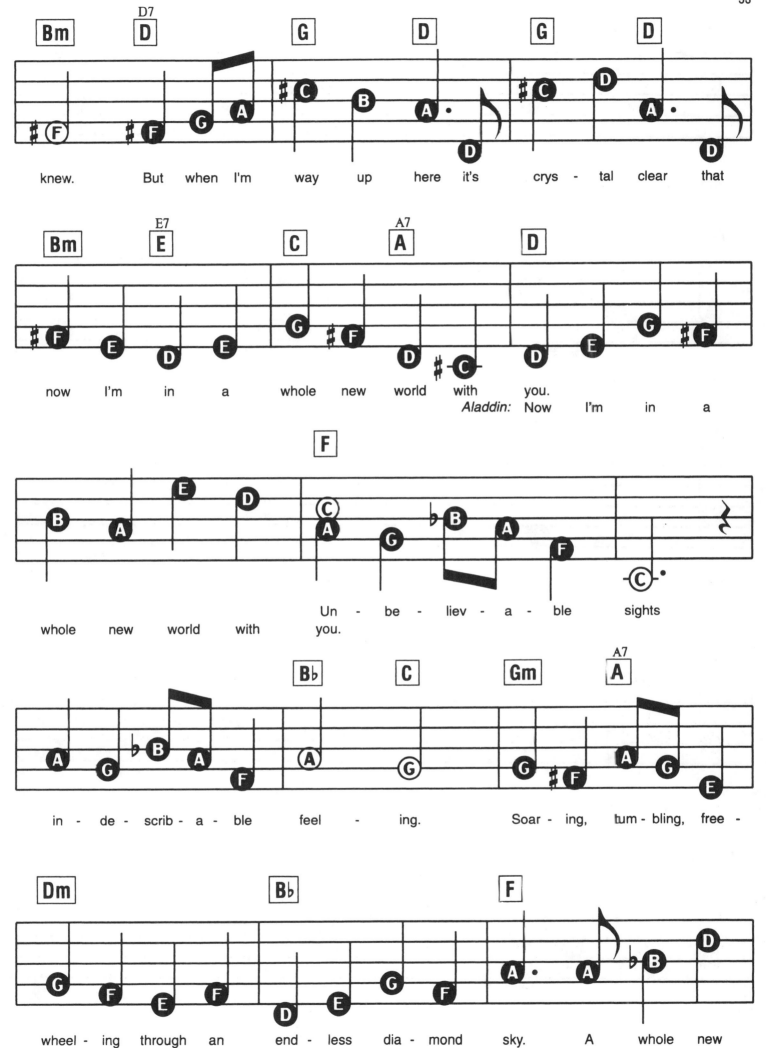

54

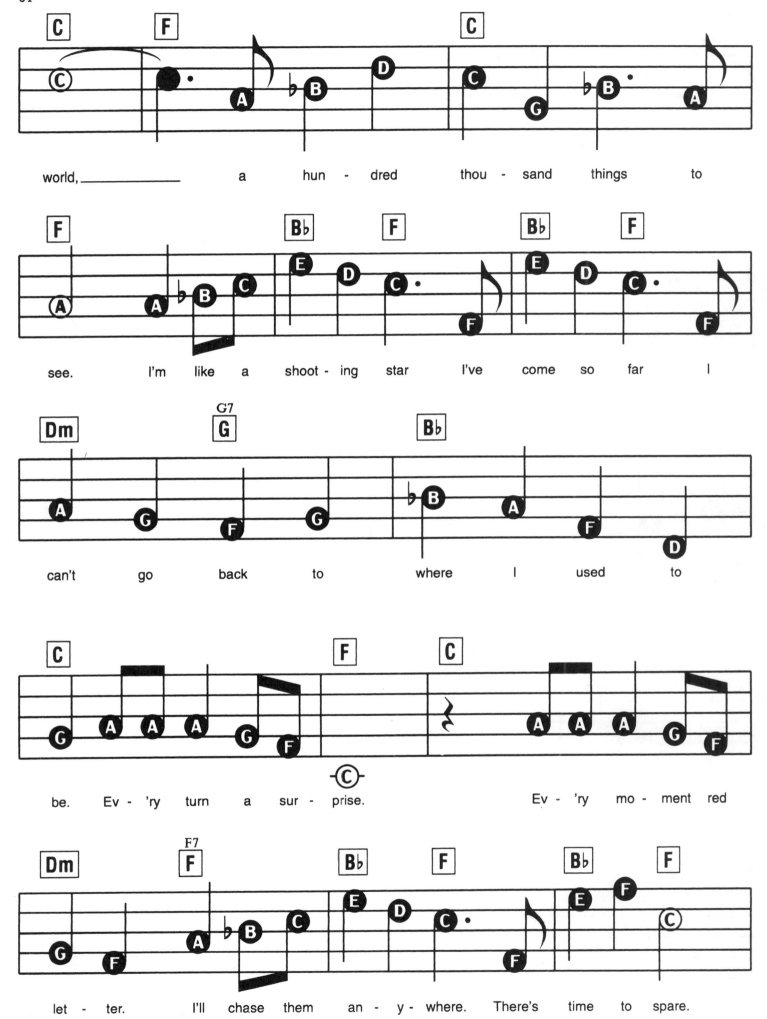

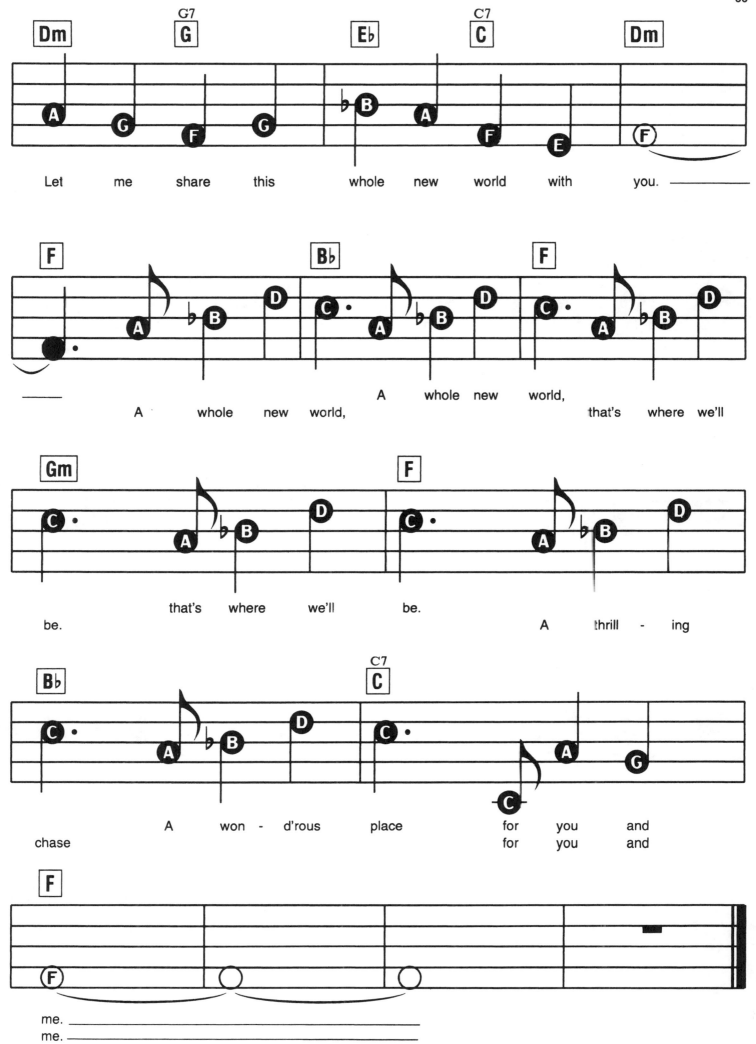

So This Is Love
from CINDERELLA

Registration 1
Rhythm: Waltz

Words and Music by Al Hoffman,
Mack David and Jerry Livingston

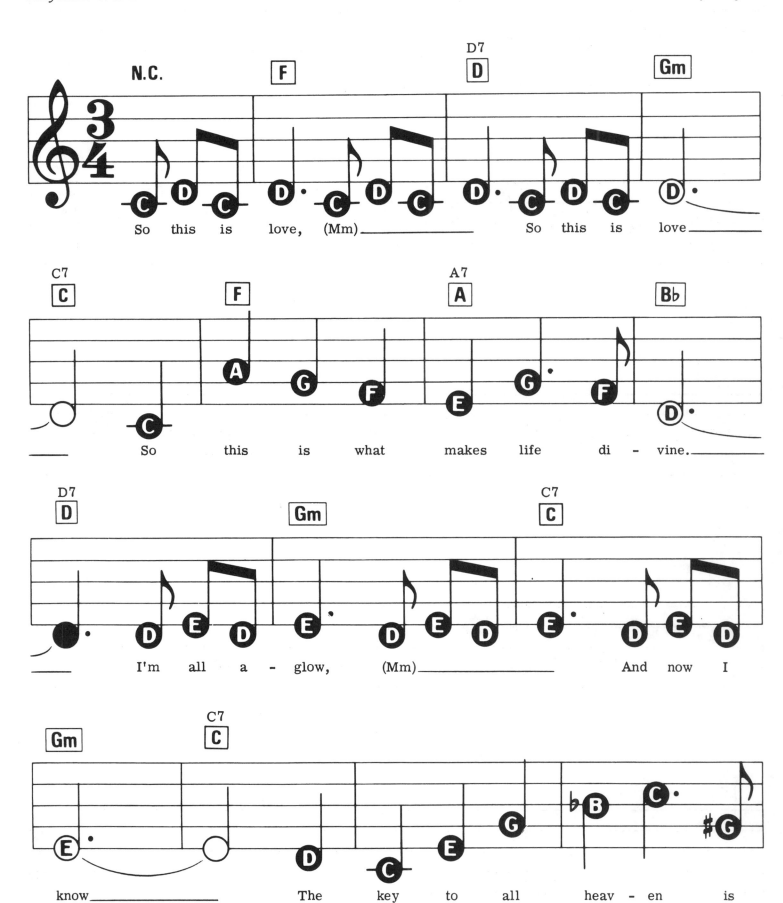

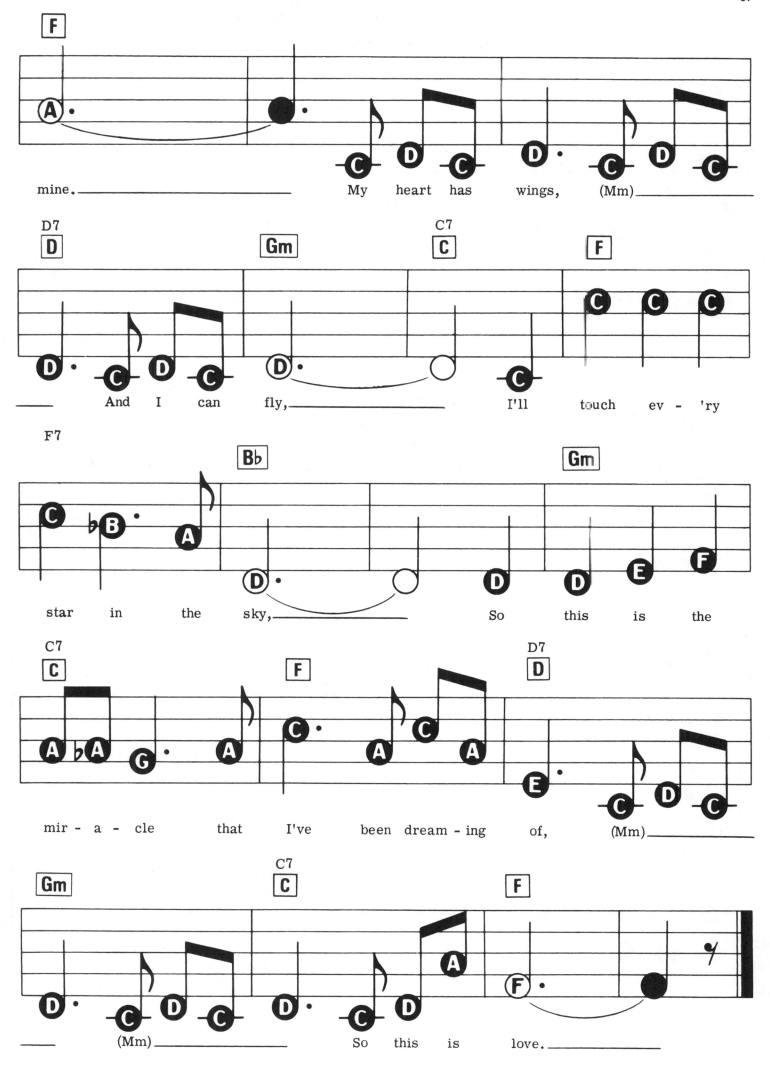

True Love's Kiss
from ENCHANTED

Registration 1
Rhythm: Broadway or Fox Trot

Music by Alan Menken
Lyrics by Stephen Schwartz

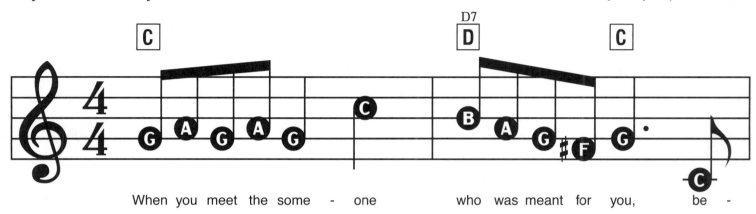

When you meet the some - one who was meant for you, be -

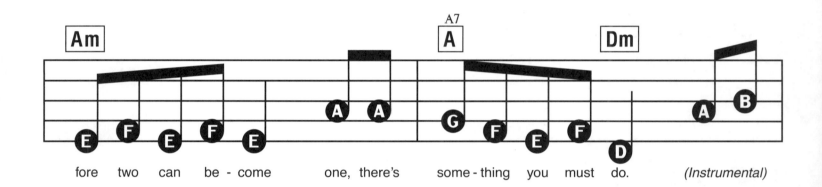

fore two can be - come one, there's some - thing you must do. *(Instrumental)*

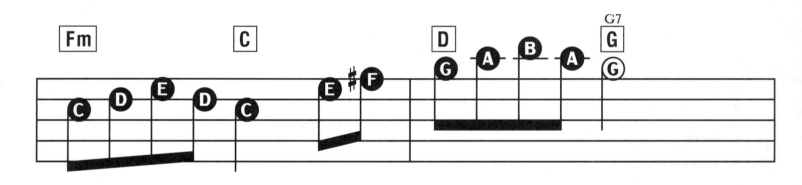

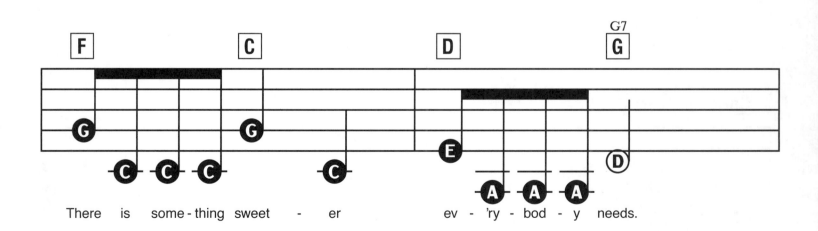

There is some - thing sweet - er ev - 'ry - bod - y needs.

59

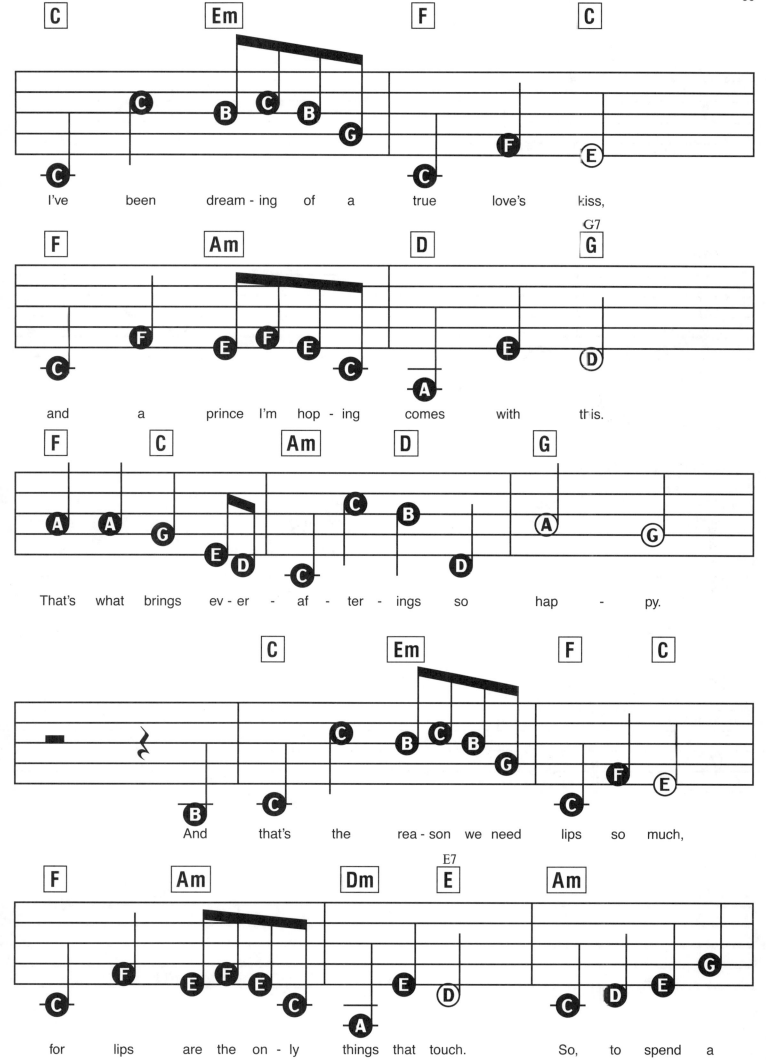

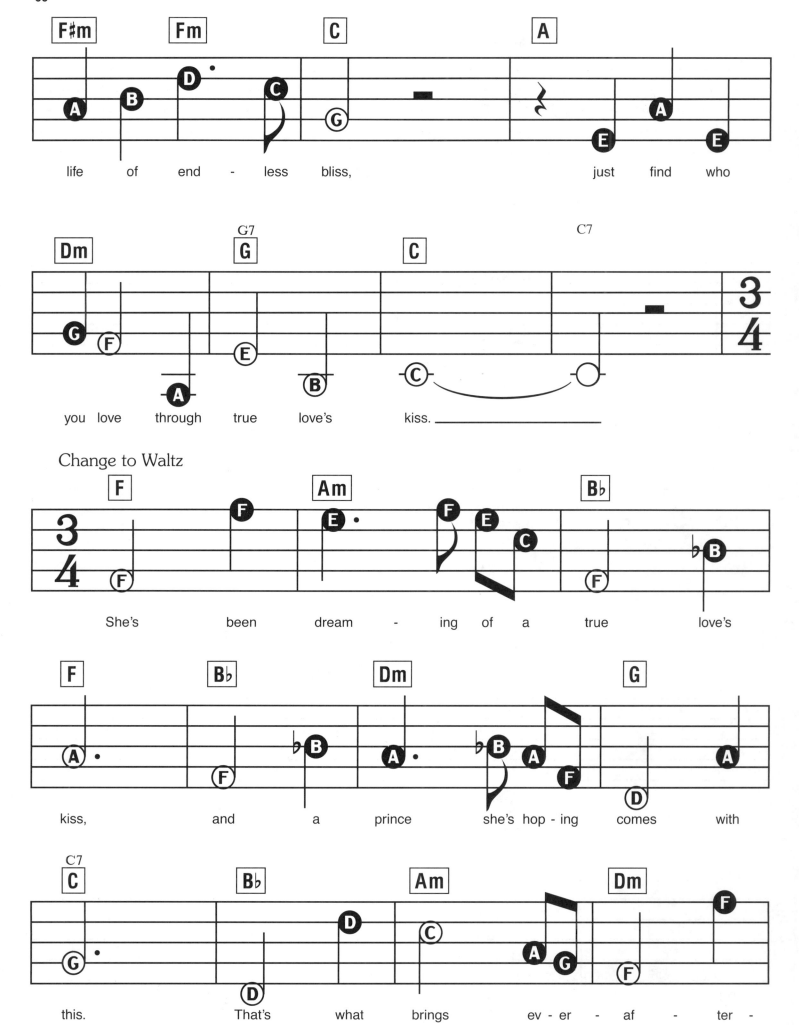

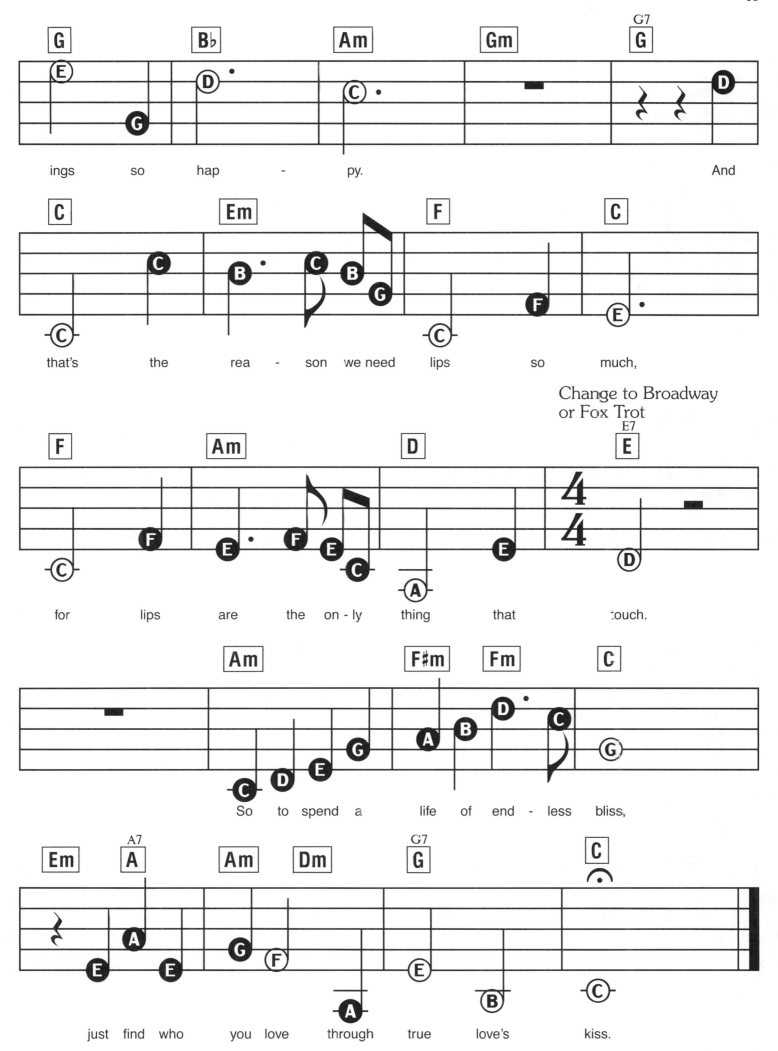

ings   so   hap - py.   And

that's   the   rea - son   we need   lips   so   much,

Change to Broadway
or Fox Trot

for   lips   are   the   on - ly   thing   that   touch.

So   to   spend   a   life   of   end - less   bliss,

just   find   who   you   love   through   true   love's   kiss.

When She Loved Me

from TOY STORY 2

Registration 8
Rhythm: Ballad

Music and Lyrics by
Randy Newman

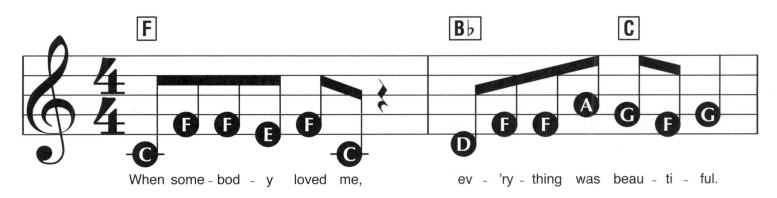

When some-bod—y loved me, ev-'ry-thing was beau-ti-ful.

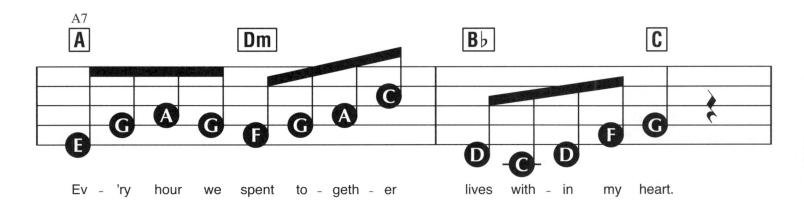

Ev—'ry hour we spent to-geth-er lives with-in my heart.

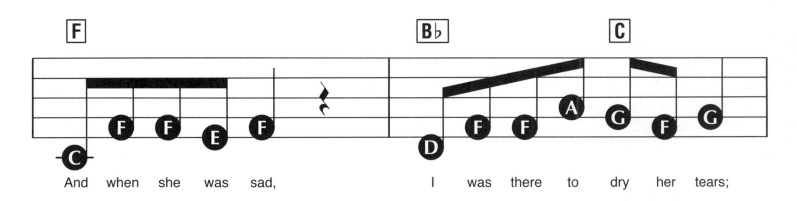

And when she was sad, I was there to dry her tears;

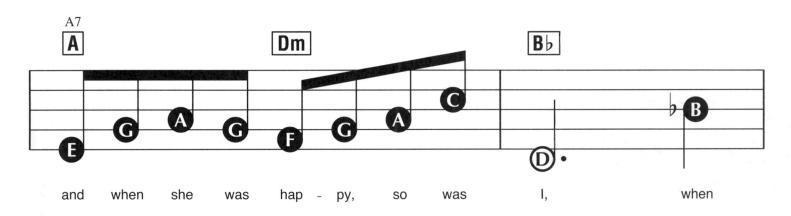

and when she was hap-py, so was I, when

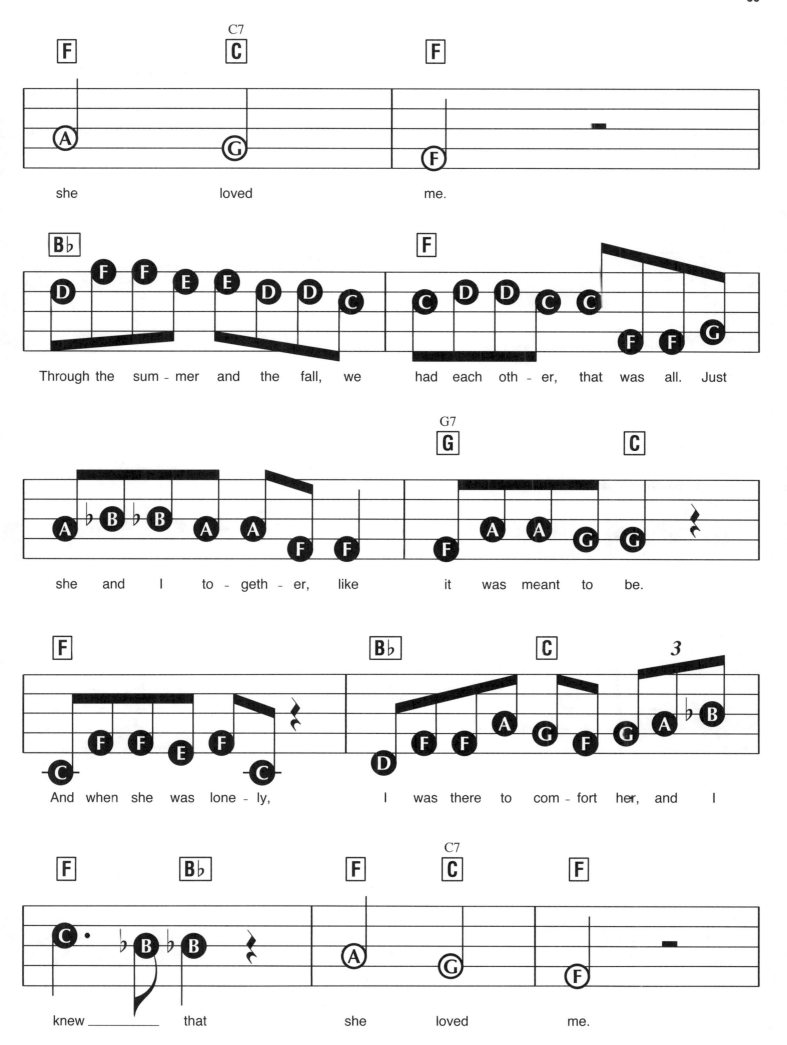

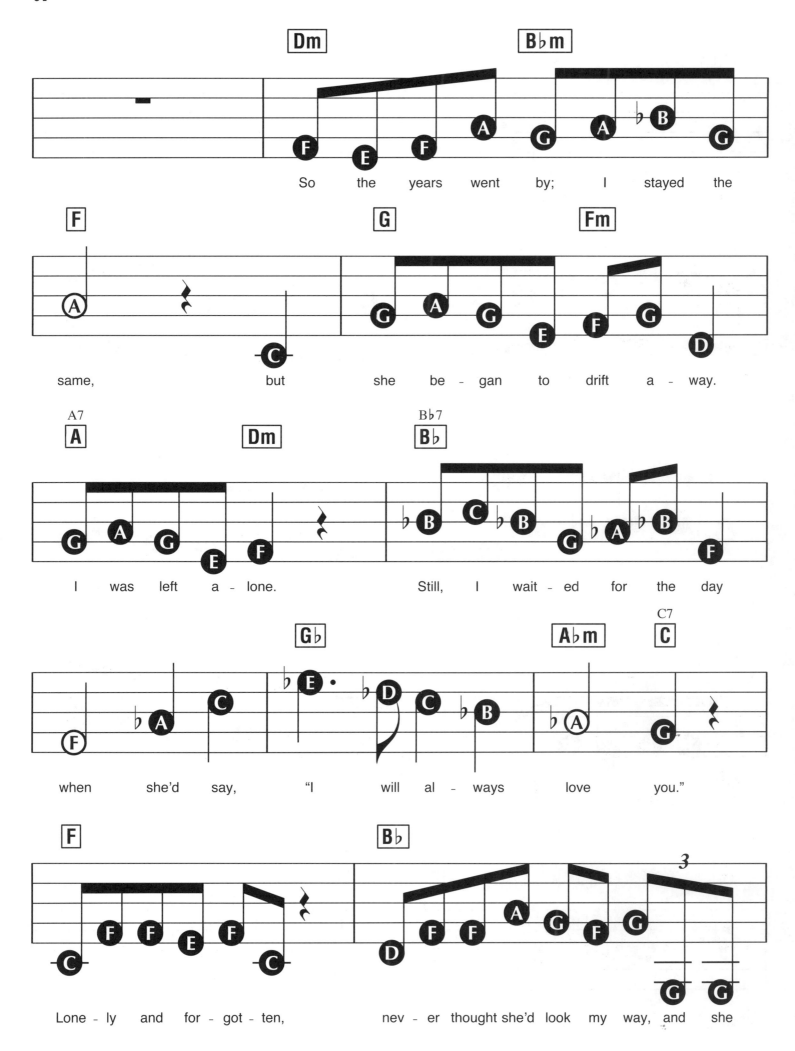

Written in the Stars
from AIDA

Registration 8
Rhythm: 8-Beat or Pops

Music by Elton John
Lyrics by Tim Rice

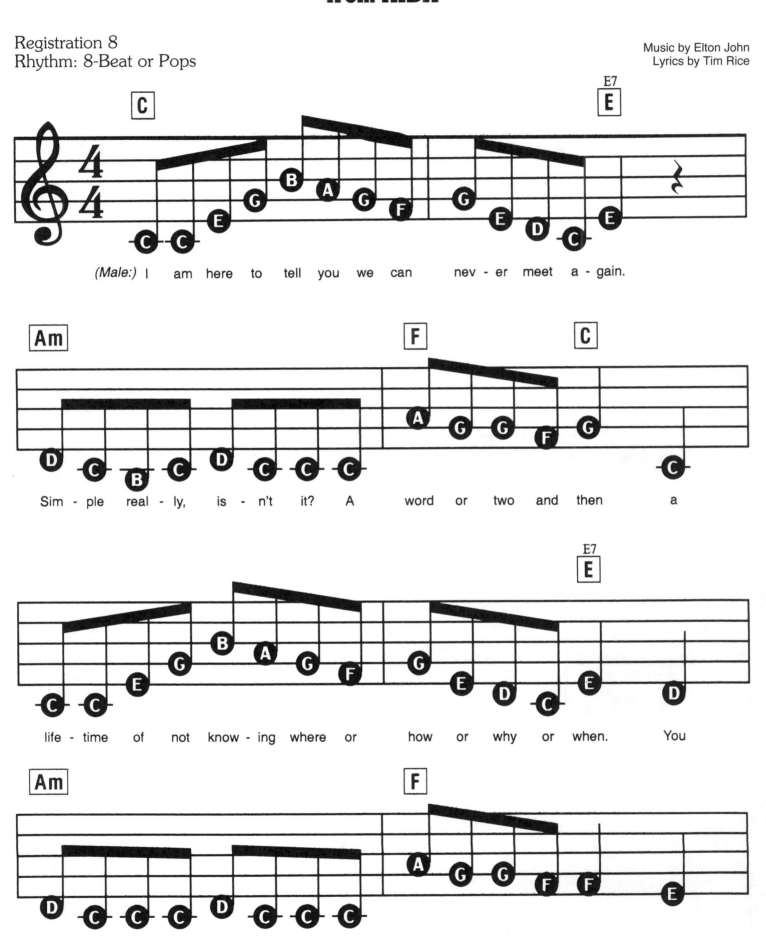

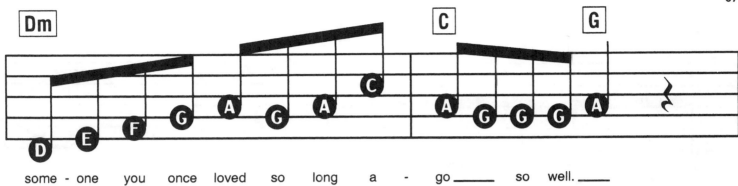

some - one you once loved so long a - go_____ so well. _____

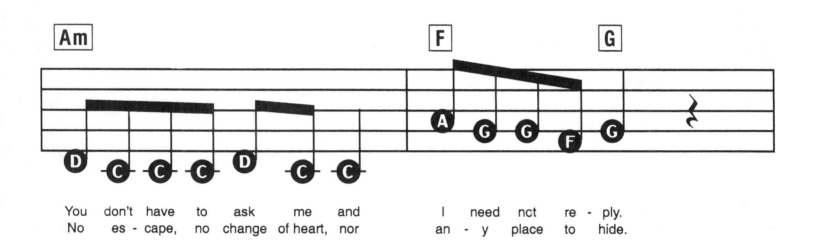

(Female:) Nev - er won - der what I'll feel_____ as liv - ing shuf - fles by.
(Male:) Noth - ing can be al - tered. Oh, there is noth - ing to de - cide.

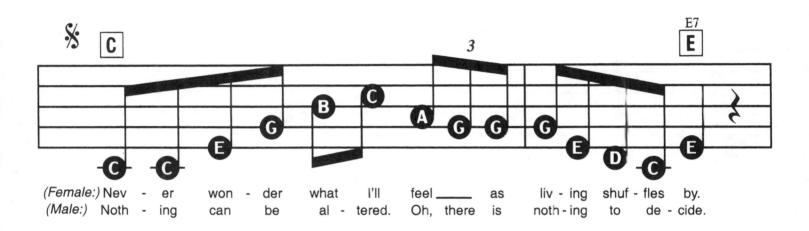

You don't have to ask me and I need nct re - ply.
No es - cape, no change of heart, nor an - y place to hide.

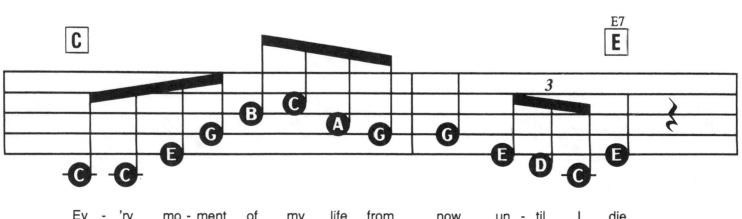

Ev - 'ry mo - ment of my life from now un - til I die
(Female:) You are all I'll ev - er want but this I am de - nied.

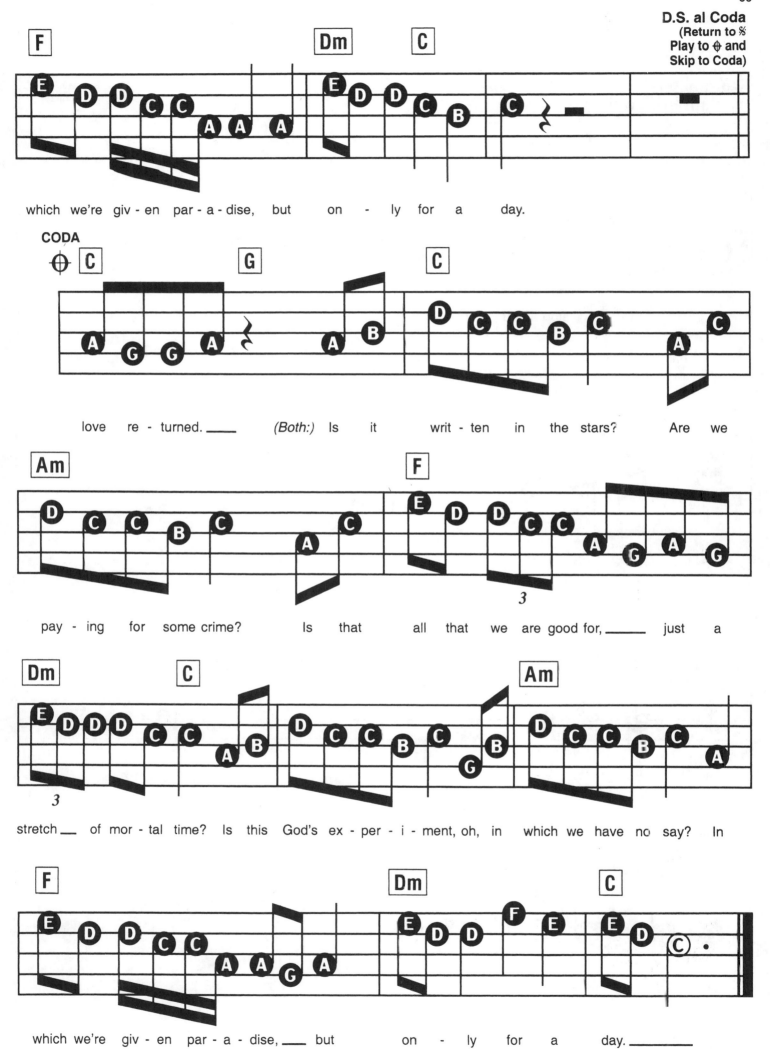

You'll Be in My Heart
from TARZAN®

Registration 3
Rhythm: Rock or Pops

Words and Music by
Phil Collins

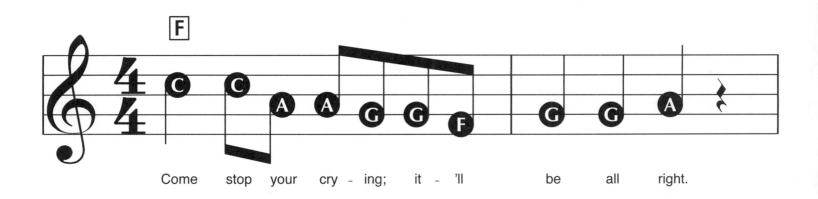

Come stop your cry - ing; it - 'll be all right.

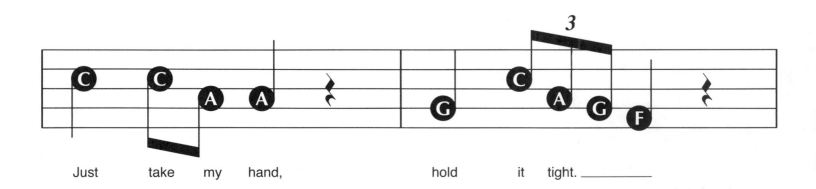

Just take my hand, hold it tight. _____

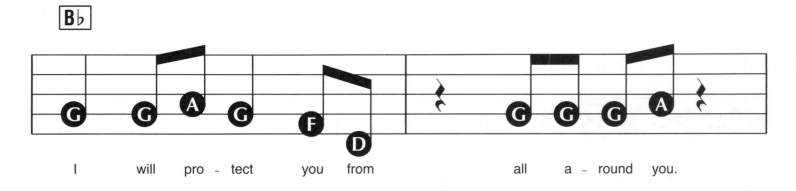

I will pro - tect you from all a - round you.

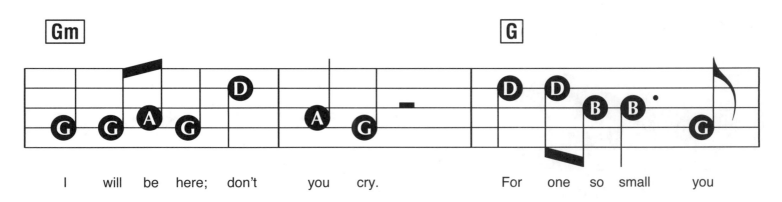

I will be here; don't you cry. For one so small you

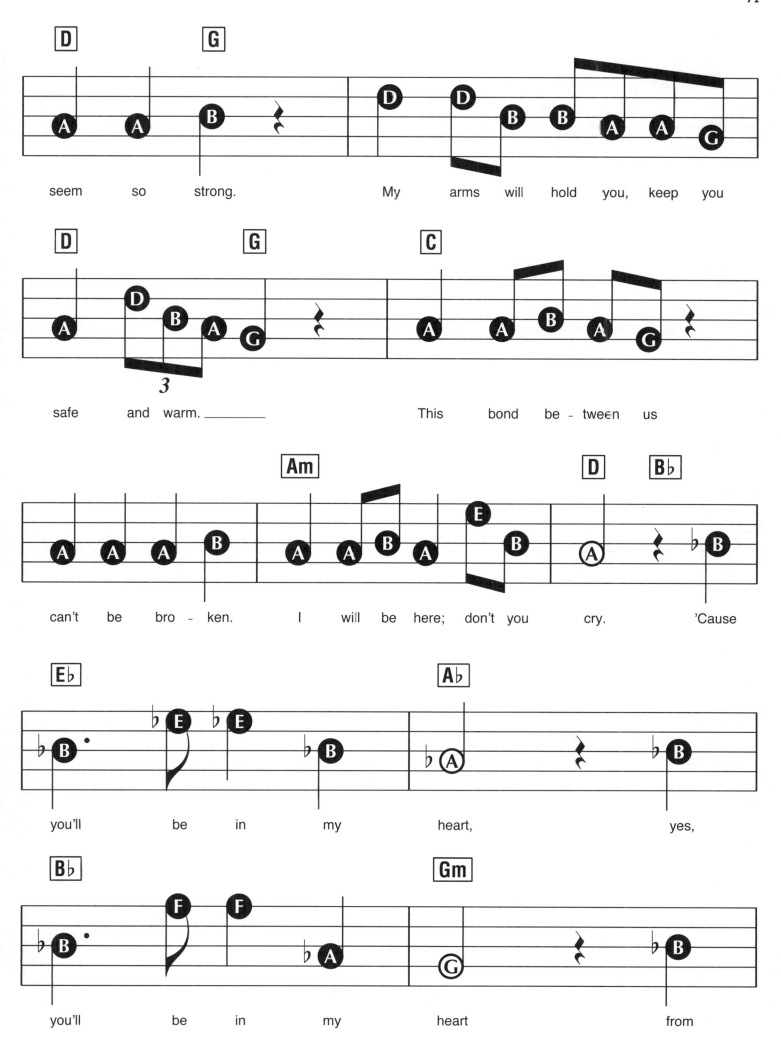

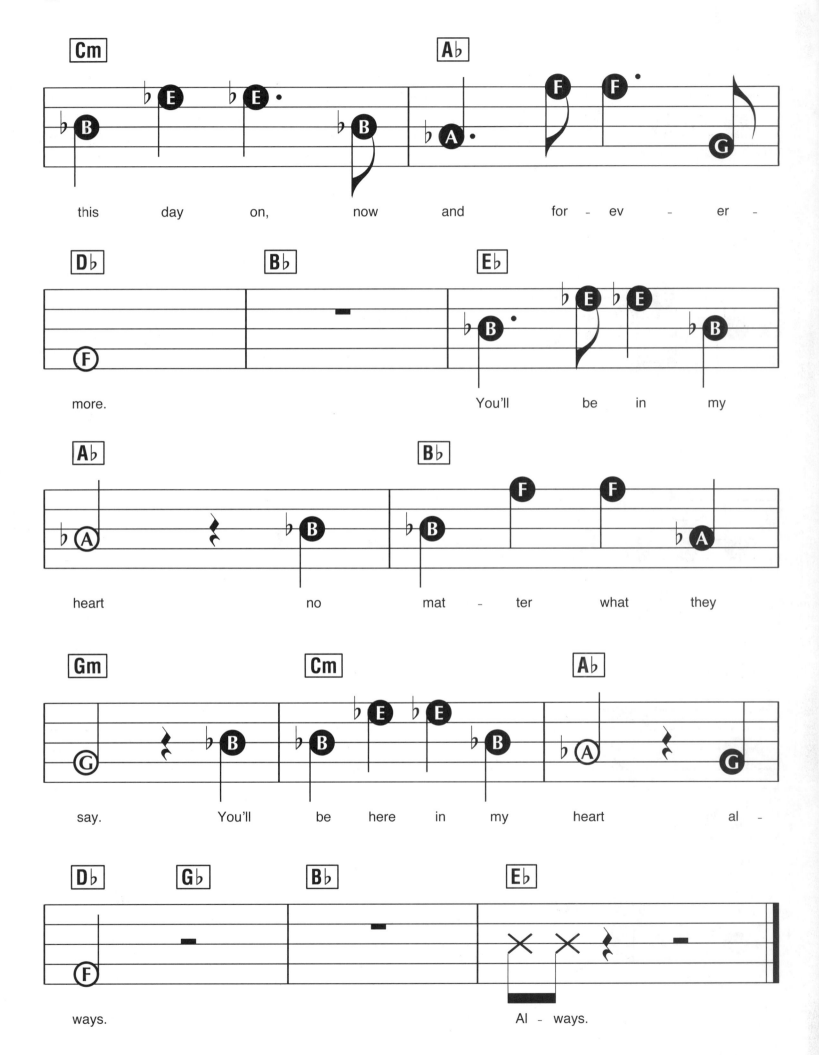